WALKING WITH SAINTS AND TINNERS

A guide to the longer routes in Cornwall

LIZ HURLEY

MUDLARK'S PRESS

Walking with Saints and Tinners
A guide to the longer routes in Cornwall

First Edition, 2022

ISBN: 978-1-913628-06-2

Maps created on Inkatlas.com. Copyright OpenStreetMap contributors (openstreetmap.org)

Cover Design: Caroline Harberd
Typesetting: Alt 19 Creative

Photography by Liz Hurley

A CIP catalogue record for this book is available from the British Library.

Mudlark's Press

www.cornishwalks.com

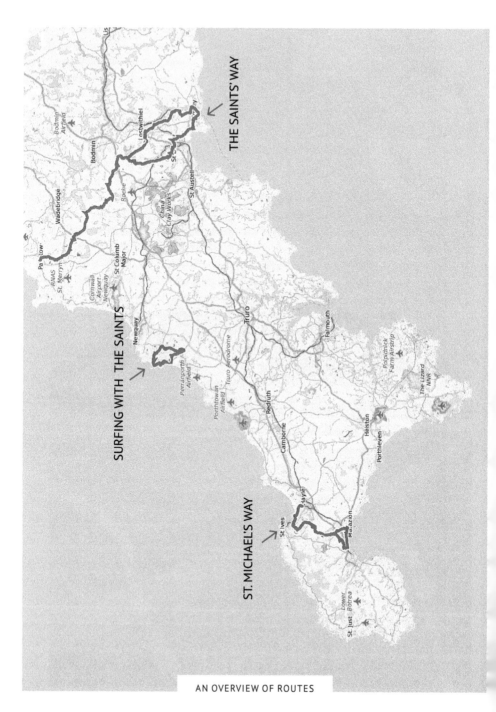

THE SAINTS' WAY

SURFING WITH THE SAINTS

ST. MICHAEL'S WAY

AN OVERVIEW OF ROUTES

CONTENTS

INTRODUCTION

Welcome to *Walking with Saints and Tinners*. This is the latest book in the Cornish Walks series and is designed to show you the very best parts of Cornwall.

The emphasis of this book is as a walking guide rather than one of pilgrimage but, naturally, this aspect of the walks will be covered too. However you enjoy your life, this book is about getting out and exploring. And, of course, there is something wonderful about getting away from the crowds and enjoying the silence around you.

These walks have been extensively tested and are widely praised for their ease of use and accuracy. However, we always recommend you carry an Ordnance Survey map with you, and a GPS app on your phone is also a useful tool.

If you do all the walks in this book and their extensions you will have walked over 120 miles. You will have walked along footpaths that have been trodden for the past four thousand years. Imagine who has been here before you: feuding giants, miners, traders fuelling the Bronze Age revolution; saints roaming the land telling others about the new religion of Christianity; farmers and drovers moving their cattle from pasture to pasture. And now you.

Each walk is accompanied by notes about various sites along the route, and these interesting snippets will help bring the walk to life. The guide also recommends great places to eat and drink locally.

At the back of the book there are some bonus features to enhance your walks, including articles on the Cornish language, the history of these paths and recommended reading.

Added Extras

In this day and age a book can only be enhanced by adding in links to further information. Each walk features useful links, a photo gallery of sights from the walk and a downloadable gpx file to accompany the walk. https://cornishwalks.com/gpx-saints/. And at the back of the book are suggestions for further reading and relevant websites.

TIPS AND ADVICE

Walking Longer Routes

The joy of these walks is that you get to explore the Cornish countryside in all its peaceful splendour, where you can go many miles without seeing another person. Shops and conveniences will also be few and far between, which makes for a great day out, but you will need a certain level of self-reliance.

- Carry a map. The maps provided in this book are for guidance only. For these distances you need to be walking with an Ordnance Survey explorer map. If you are using the map on a phone app, ensure your phone is fully charged and be sure to carry a charger and lead. The number of times I leave the lead in the car is embarrassing.

- Take food and water with you. You can't guarantee that the café ahead will be open.

- Loos. These are few and far between. Pubs and cafés will always let you use theirs if they are open and you are a patron.

- Pack a second pair of socks. Always. Damp socks cause blisters.

- Take plasters, just in case.

- Wear comfortable clothes. Thin layers are best as you can whip these on and off.

- Know your limits. It's hard to get too lost in Cornwall, but if it's raining, visibility is awful and your legs are aching, turn around. The walk will always be there another day. Walking should be fun, not an ordeal.

Distance

There's also no obligation to walk the entire section. Just find a bit that sounds interesting and walk a 'there and back' section. I think the following shorter sections are great walks in their own right, and each is only a few miles there and back.

- Ludgvan to Marazion via the marshes
- Luxulyan to Viaduct
- Lanlivery to Helman Tor
- Lankelly to Polkerris
- Padstow to Little Petherick
- Lelant to Carbis Bay

The Countryside Code

- Respect the people who live and work in the countryside. Respect private property, farmland and all rural environments.

- Do not interfere with livestock, machinery and crops.

- Respect and, where possible, protect all wildlife, plants and trees.

- When walking, use the approved routes and keep as closely as possible to them.

- Take special care when walking on country roads.

- Leave all gates as you find them and do not interfere with or damage any gates, fences, walls or hedges.

- Guard against all risks of fire, especially near forests.

- Always keep children closely supervised while on a walk.

- Do not walk the Ways in large groups and always maintain a low profile.

- Take all litter home, leaving only footprints behind.

- Keep the number of cars used to the minimum and park carefully to avoid blocking farm gateways or narrow roads.

- Minimise impact on fragile vegetation and soft ground.

- Take heed of warning signs – they are there for your protection.

Cattle

By and large, a herd of cattle will cause no harm. They are used to walkers and are likely to ignore you unless you draw attention to yourself. If you find yourself in a field of suddenly wary cattle, move away as carefully and quietly as possible, and if you feel threatened by cattle then let go of your dog's lead and let it run free rather than try to protect it and endanger yourself. The dog will outrun the cows, and it will also outrun you.

Those without canine companions should follow similar advice: move away calmly, do not panic and make no sudden noises. Chances are the cows will leave you alone once they establish that you pose no threat.

If you walk through a field of cows and there happens to be calves please be vigilant, as mothers can be more protective. If crossing a field with cattle in, you don't need to stick to the footpath if you wish to avoid them. By all means skirt around the edge of the field.

Remain quiet. Cows are curious, and if they hear a lot of noise they will come over to investigate.

GUIDE TO THE ROUTES

Before heading off for a walk, read the description first, as you may discover issues with it, e.g. cows, tides, number of stiles or mud. Then have a look at a map – not just the little one provided with the walk – to get a proper feel for the direction of the walk.

Length: This has been calculated using a range of GPS tracking devices but, ultimately, we have used the Ordnance Survey route tracker. This will generally differ from an inbuilt phone pedometer.

Effort: None of these walks are difficult, just long. There will, however, be plenty of hills.

Terrain: If it's been raining a lot, please assume that footpaths will be muddy. Towards the end of summer, vegetation may obscure the paths and signposts. The routes are mainly a mixture of paths and small lanes.

Livestock: You are likely to meet cows, sheep and horses. Please read the Countryside Code section on how to walk through livestock.

WCs: Due to council cuts, many loos are now closed or run by local parishes with seasonal opening hours. If they are an essential part of your walk, check online first. Many are now coin operated.

Cafés/Pubs: Always check ahead, as some will have seasonal opening hours.

Points of Information: To avoid duplication of text, all Points of Interest are at the end of the walk, described both ways. As you read the instructions, bold text indicates further information.

GPX Files: https://cornishwalks.com/gpx-saints/

FINALLY
Things change: trees fall down, posts get broken, signs become obscured and footpaths can be closed for repair. Don't be alarmed if you can't see a marker, but do check your map and see if everything else is in order.

GENERAL POINTS OF INTEREST

History of the Paths

In the beginning there was tin, Cornish tin. Long before the Roman Empire, and long before the rise of Christianity, there was the tin and copper trade. Tin and copper are the two components of bronze and were, therefore, essential in powering the Bronze Age. Cornwall was rich in both, making it an essential trade centre. Tin mining began in Cornwall circa 2000 BC, making this a 4,000-year-old trade. There is evidence of two main routes crossing Cornwall, connecting Wales and Ireland with Europe. Sailing around the tip of Cornwall was treacherous, so a land bridge was safer.

Various early Bronze Age gold necklaces found in Ireland were made using Cornish gold. The Nebra Sky Disc, made circa 1600 BC and found in Germany, is a Bronze Age artefact made with Cornish tin. This is all evidence that Cornish metals were being traded all across Europe.

These routes were clearly well traced, and during the golden Age of Saints, from the fifth to seventh centuries AD, these routes were once again in use. During this period, holy men and women were spreading the Christian message from the Western Isles of Scotland through Ireland, across Wales, then through Cornwall and onto Brittany and the rest of Europe. Sailing around the tip of Cornwall continued to be hazardous, and why bother when such well-established routes were already in place?

Fast forward to the twentieth century, when various walking groups decided to resurrect these old routes using historical records, Cornish crosses and conjecture to map out new routes. The Saints' Way was established by Michael Gill and Derek Millar in the 1980s. It is also known in Cornish as the *Forth an Syns*. The St Michael's Way was re-established in 1994. Both paths are regularly walked and are maintained by Cornwall Council. The Ramblers Association also take care of sections of the path at a local level.

Pilgrimage

Both routes can be walked as part of the Camino pilgrimage: the famous European pilgrimage to Santiago de Compostela, Santiago being Spanish for St James. As you walk along the paths, keep an eye out for scallop shells, the symbol of St James.

If you wish to record your route using pilgrim stamps, you will find them in the following locations.

St Michael's Way

Pilgrim Record available via https://www.csj.org.uk/shop You can use this passport for both routes and all the way to Santiago de Compostela in Spain. (Small fee.)

- **Lelant:** Inside St Uny's Church, near the St Michael's Way banner.

- **Bowl Rock:** By the gate of Tresithney, which is the house on the right (from the Lelant direction) leading down to Bowl Rock.

- **Trencrom Hill:** On the waymark post by the kissing-gate adjacent to the road entrance of the National Trust Trencrom Hill Car Park.

- **Ludgvan:** Inside the church, near the St Michael's Way banner.

- **Gulval (optional):** In the entrance porch of the Coldstreamer Inn, which is just beyond Gulval Church and opens at 11am. Follow the road to the right around the churchyard and the Inn is ahead on the left. Continue down around the churchyard to rejoin the St Michael's Way route on the right.

- **Marazion:** Inside the church, near the St Michael's Way banner.

- **St Michael's Mount:** In the Change House, which is open from 8am to 6pm during the season (mid-March to the end of Oct/start of Nov). Ask the staff on duty for the St Michael's Way stamp.

The Saints' Way

Pilgrim Record available via https://trurodiocese.org.uk/faith-life/pilgrimages/ Click on **Saints' Way Passport PDF (free). Doesn't include the St Michael's Way.**

- St Petroc's Church, Padstow
- Lanivet Church, Lanivet
- St Cyriacus & St Julitta Church, Luxulyan
- St Petroc Minor Church, Little Petherick
- St Brevita Church, Lanlivery
- St Blaise Church, St Blazey
- St Issey Church, St Issey
- St Bartholomew's Church, Lostwithiel
- St Andrew's Church, Tywardreath
- St Clement's Church, Withiel
- St Sampson's Church, Golant
- Fowey Museum, Fowey

THE SAINTS' WAY

The Saints' Way is a wonderful long walk connecting the north and south coasts of Cornwall, from Padstow in the north, to Fowey in the south. It is often walked over two days using Lanivet as the halfway point. The path is well signed and maintained but generally quiet, and you can often walk the route without seeing another walker once you leave the coastal sections.

The northern half of the walk crosses St Breock Downs, a high open space with glorious views in all directions, including magnificent stretches along the Camel Estuary as you wind your way along creek-side paths heading towards Padstow.

The southern half of the walk splits east and west. Taking the eastern route you head up along Helman Tor, a spectacular granite outcrop, and then on until you are walking through land full of Arthurian legends.

Taking the western route you get the opportunity to explore the jaw-dropping Treffry Viaduct and a landscape dominated by industrial archaeology, giant boulders and tiny streams. There is also an option to take a detour and walk the last (or first) few miles along the coast path, exploring little beaches and spectacular views. This adds another two miles to your journey.

Occasionally, I will offer detours from the main route to avoid issues such as traffic or cattle, or to offer better views or points of interest.

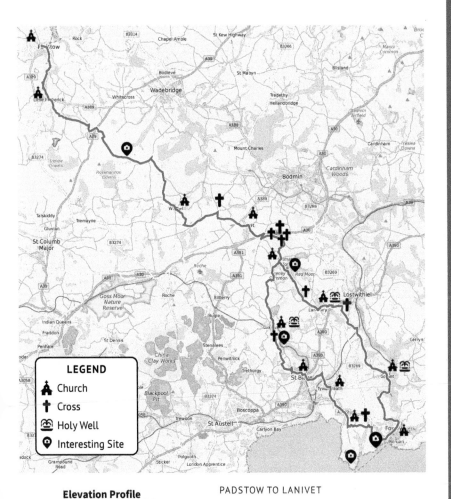

Elevation Profile — PADSTOW TO LANIVET

Elevation Profile — LANIVET TO FOWEY - EAST ELEVATION

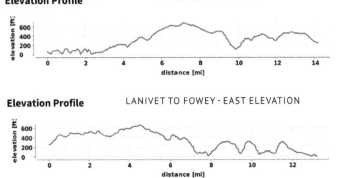

PADSTOW TO LANIVET
North to South

OS Maps: 106 / 107

WCs: Padstow– All facilities. No further facilities until Lanivet

Length: 14.5 miles

Link: https://cornishwalks.com/gpx-saints/

DIRECTIONS:

0–2.5 miles: Padstow to Little Petherick

1. From **Saint Petroc's Church** take the lychgate out of the graveyard and head off on the footpath. When you reach a collection of road junctions, cross over to Dennis Road. Walk down Dennis Road and then continue along Dennis Lane. You are heading in the direction of the obelisk on the horizon. As the road peters out, turn left along Dennis Cove and up to a metal gate.

2. Go through the gate and keep to the right-hand side of the field. At the top of the field head through the gap in the stone wall, over some granite steps and into another field. Turn immediately left and with the hedge on your left-hand side, walk downhill into the next field. Continue downhill, cutting across the middle of the field, heading towards the river. At the bottom of the field turn right at the hedge and walk alongside the hedge until you reach a path on the

PADSTOW TO A39

13

left heading downhill through the trees; take this turning.

3. Follow the path down and across the creek then back up into a field, keeping to the right-hand side. Cross the stile into the next field and continue, keeping to the left-hand side of this field. Follow the path along the next field until you start heading downhill and cross over a larger creek. When the path heads up, at the top of the path walk into the field and follow the stone hedge, bearing right, then cross a wooden stile into the woods.

Follow the path down towards a small collection of creek-side holiday cottages and walk through the complex until you get to the road. The church of **St Petroc Minor** is to your right.

2.5–5 miles: Little Petherick to the A39

4. Turn left over the bridge. You then need to walk up the road before taking the path on the right-hand side. This is a fast road with no footpath, so be aware of the traffic. The Saints' Way starts again just after the cream house; step off the road and continue up the path to a wooden gate and then down a concrete drive. Near the bottom of the drive take the left-hand path. Head through the gate and along the bottom of the field. The path ends at a house driveway. Follow the drive up onto a small lane. Turn right on the lane and start walking along the road, passing Mellingey Mill.

5. Stay on this road for just under a mile until you reach a hamlet. Pass a phone box and a grit bin then take the left-hand turning. Stay on the private lane for half a mile as it gradually turns into a footpath until you reach a kissing-gate. Head through the gate into farmland, sticking to the right-hand side, cross the next stile and then walk directly across the next field. Turn right, heading downhill towards the small stream, then take the bridge across and climb up through the middle of the next field. Head across the middle of the next field, walking towards the buildings and keeping them just to your right.

6. Pass through the wooden kissing-gate into a holiday farm complex. Walk along the drive until you reach the road. Turn right and walk until you get to a T-junction. Turn left and follow the road until it reaches the A39.

5–7.5 miles: The A39 to St Breock Downs

7. Cross the A39, taking care, and then head down the small road to West Park Farm. Follow this lane through the trees and then back up into farmland. There are often lots of game birds in this field so make sure your dogs are on a lead. As you get into the field, keep the hedge on your left and head uphill. In the next field continue uphill but now keeping the hedge on your right.

8. Cross the stile into the next field then turn sharp left and follow the hedge. Leave

the field via a wooden stile, onto a small path that turns into a private road. Walk along this road for a mile. Nearing the end of this section, as you come alongside the large white turbines on your left-hand side there is a dilapidated house by the concrete road. To the right, just a few steps off the road, is the **St Breock Longstone**. Explore, then come back onto the road. Continue along the road as it joins a main road, now turn left. You are now back on the public highway. Shortly after this you reach another junction.

7.5–10.5 miles: St Breock Downs to Withiel

9. Turn left and head down the road. Ignore the first right-hand turning to St Wenn and then take the second right-hand turning to Hustyns.

10. After half a mile the road bends sharply to the right then, as it bends to the left, you leave the road and walk forward along a grass path towards a gate and a wind turbine. Head into the field and stick to the left-hand side, passing through the

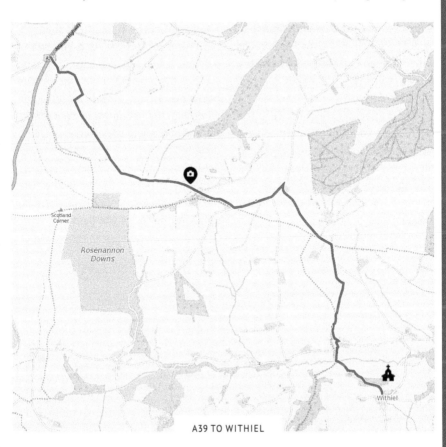

A39 TO WITHIEL

gate into the next field, where the wind turbine is. You need to make your way to the bottom right corner of this very large field. At the bottom right there is a gate and stile. You won't see the exit straight away due to the size of the field, but just start walking downhill. If there are cattle in the field, choose any route. Leave the field via the stile and head down the track.

11. Where the track comes down to meet a road, turn right, following the road downhill as it bends to the left. From here you can see **St Clement's Church** in the distance. Follow the road as it bends to the right, and just after the bend the footpath turns left into a field.

12. Walking across the field, keep the tree in the middle of the field to your left, and head down towards a wooden stile. (If you wish to avoid this field keep walking down the road, take the first left-hand track and head down to the bridge.)

13. Turn left after the stile and take the wooden bridge across the stream. This is a very pretty spot. Take the path uphill and turn left, following the half mile sign to Withiel. Follow this path up through the trees and then onto a tarmac track heading uphill. This section is quite steep. At the top of the track, as you reach the church, turn left and then, as you get to a road, turn right. Walk past the front of the church and head out of the village.

10.5–13 miles: Withiel to Higher Woodley

14. Just after the agricultural shed, the path turns left off the road. Follow the path into a field and then cross it, heading towards the telegraph pole that is in the hedgerow. Walk underneath the telegraph wires with the hedgerow on your left. At the end of the field take the path heading downhill through a thicket. In the lower field, cross a small stream and then cross a granite stile into the bottom of the next field. Walk straight ahead, heading uphill. At the top of the field turn right,

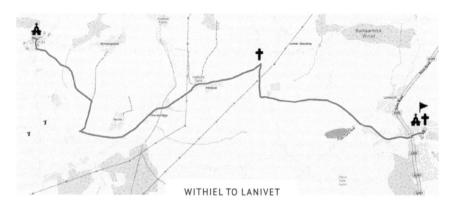

WITHIEL TO LANIVET

following the hedgerow, and then leave the field via a stile, following the footpath into the next field.

15. You now need to cut directly across the field. Ignore the big gap in the hedgerow opposite but look further along to your left-hand side. There is a finger post in the hedge and a small spindly tree – this is your exit point. Climb over the stile and turn right, walking up a broad track.

16. When the track joins a road, turn left. You will be on this road for the next two miles, following the Saints' Way finger posts at each junction. When you come to the crossroads where you turn right, look over to your left for a granite cross. Now, just as the road turns sharp right in front of Higher Woodley Farm, take the stile directly ahead of you.

13–14.5 miles: Higher Woodley to Lanivet

17. Keep to the left-hand side of the field. Cross the next three fields until you walk between two hedgerows and rejoin a road. Turn right and start walking downhill. Cross a main road and head down Clann Lane into the village of Lanivet. Head towards **Lanivet Church**, where this walk ends.

LANIVET TO PADSTOW
South to North

OS Maps: 106 / 107

WCs: Lanivet– All facilities. No further facilities until Padstow

Length: 14.5 miles

Link: https://cornishwalks.com/gpx-saints/

DIRECTIONS:

0–1.5 miles: Lanivet to Higher Woodley

1. From the front of **Lanivet Church**, walk down to the main road and take Clann Lane, opposite the Lanivet Inn. Walk up until you reach a crossroads then continue uphill, passing the recycling centre on your left. As the road turns sharp right, leave the road and walk straight ahead going through the gate. Follow the path into a field, keeping to the right-hand side. At the far end, enter the next field and walk directly across the middle of it, pass through the gate and then stick to the right-hand side of the next field until you come out at Higher Woodley Farm.

1.5–4 miles: Higher Woodley to Withiel

2. Walk straight ahead onto the road and continue until you reach the T-junction. Just over to your right, across the junction, is a stone cross in the hedgerow. Turn left at the T-junction and walk for a mile until you reach the right-hand junction

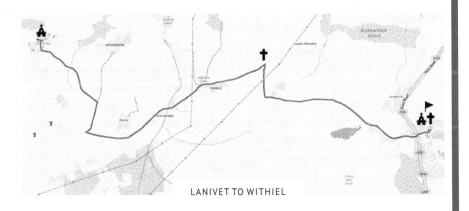

LANIVET TO WITHIEL

21

to Retire. Take the second right and head uphill along the small lane. There is a Saints' Way signpost. At the top of the hill, as the road bends to the left, the path now turns right, off onto a rough track.

3. Follow the track until you reach a gap in the hedge on both sides. Take the left-hand path. Climb over the stile into the field and then walk directly across it towards the gate on the other side.

4. Cross the stile into the next field and keep to the right-hand side of the field; as you pass a gate you now need to cut across the field heading downhill and towards the trees on the opposite side. The exit is obvious when you're halfway across the field: you can see the stile in the hedgerow.

5. Take the little bridge across the stream, then in the next field head uphill through the copse into the upper field and head towards the church. To exit this field, head to the telegraph pole in the hedgerow and then cut straight across the field to the gate on the other side.

6. Follow the path up onto the road and turn right, heading into the village of Withiel. Pass **St Clement's Church** and then take the left-hand turning just after the bus shelter. Just after the graveyard take the track on your right, following the signs to Blackhay Farm.

4–7 miles: Withiel to St Breock Downs

7. Head down the concrete drive until you reach two granite gateposts without a gate. Take the track on the right just before them and continue down through the trees until you reach the valley floor. Cross the ford via the wooden bridge and then cross the stile. Directly ahead of you, across the field, you'll see your exit stile. Leave the field then turn right onto a road and head uphill. Turn left in front of Tregustick Barn and continue uphill along a long steep track that ends at a gate.

8. Head into the field. This is a very large field and your exit is at the far top right. There are often cattle in this field, so choose any path you wish that you feel comfortable with. Keep heading in the direction of the wind turbine until you can see the exit gate. In the next field, keep to the hedgerow on your right. Exit via a kissing-gate and walk towards the road.

9. At the road, turn left and stay on this road for just under a mile, passing Hustyns on your right, until the T-junction. Turn left and walk for another half mile until you reach a right-hand turn signposted to **St Breock Monolith** (also known as the St Breock Longstone). Take this turn and, soon after, take another right-hand turning. As you approach a derelict breezeblock building, the monolith is just off the road to your left.

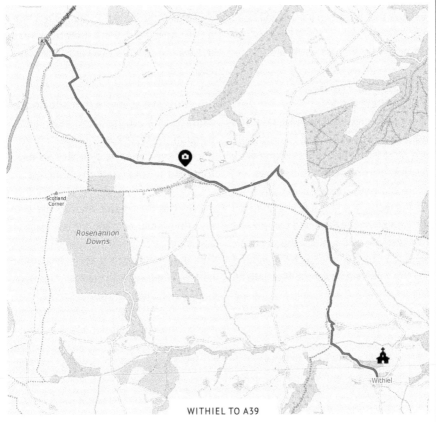

WITHIEL TO A39

7–9.5 miles: St Breock Downs to the A39

10. Having explored the monolith, come back to the road and continue straight ahead as it becomes an unmade lane. Stay on this lane for just under a mile. You will pass through two ornamental stone gateposts; continue until you get to a second pair and then take the footpath to the right of the stone post. As you walk along this lane you will get your first glimpse of the sea. **Padstow** is nestled to the left side of the estuary mouth.

11. Head down the path and into a field, keeping to the right-hand side. Exit at the far right and continue along the right-hand side of the next field, heading downhill. Halfway down the field turn right at the gate and cross the stile. Keep the hedge to your left. As you get to the bottom of the field there is a meeting of several fields. Walk forwards, keeping the scrappy-looking hedge to your right-hand side, and head downhill. At the bottom of this field the path leads into an unmade track; head downhill on this track. Follow

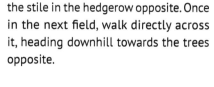

this track as it becomes a drive and head up to the junction of the A39. This is a fast, busy road – cross with care.

9.5–12 miles: The A39 to Little Petherick

12. Having crossed the A39, take the small lane opposite and head uphill. Turn right at the first junction and walk downhill, passing several properties. Just before the road turns steeply downhill take the footpath on the left, heading onto a private driveway. Pass by a complex of farm cottages and holiday lets, through the gate at the far end of the drive and into the field. Head across the field to the stile in the hedgerow opposite. Once in the next field, walk directly across it, heading downhill towards the trees opposite.

13. Cross the stile and then the bridge over the small stream. Now head uphill through the little copse of trees, to the edge of the upper field. Cross this field towards the small gate in the hedge.

14. In the next field, stick to the left and then head through a kissing-gate and along a footpath. Follow this track for half a mile until it ends at a small hamlet. When you join the road turn right and head downhill through the hamlet. Just beyond the hamlet take the left-hand lane, heading briefly uphill. Stay on this road all the way down to Mellingey Mill.

15. Continue past the mill and through the hamlet, and as the road begins to rise again take the footpath off to the left-hand side, just after the last bungalow. Follow the footpath all the way down to Little Petherick. Do not join the road too soon – make sure you take the path that runs beside the road behind a hedge. You will need to walk a small section on the road, so take care.

A39 TO PADSTOW

12–14.5 miles: Little Petherick to Padstow

16. Cross the bridge, and just before **St Petroc Minor Church** take the turning to the right. As the private lane turns into a track, follow the signs for the Saints' Way and head up into the woods. As the path enters a field, keep to the top-right edge and walk towards the next section of woods. The path down to the creek is steep and poorly signed, but head downhill and keep to the left. Zigzag down if needs be.

17. Now take the boardwalk across the creek and head up on the other side. Follow the path through a few fields, keeping to the right-hand side. The path leads down to another creek crossing – cross over then head uphill on a left-hand diagonal. Keep the obelisk to your right and take the footpath through the right-hand hedge. You don't visit the obelisk, but if you want to explore make sure to come back to this point. Now head down the field, keeping the hedge on your left until you come to a private drive.

18. Follow the drive until it becomes Dennis Lane. Walk forward, heading for the bungalows straight ahead. At the top of the lane turn right and walk along Dennis Road. At the next junction cross the road, turn left, cross the next road and then walk down Hill Street. Follow this road until it becomes a footpath and then follow the path to **St Petroc's Church**. This is the end of your walk. Congratulations.

THE SAINTS' WAY: POINTS OF INTEREST

Granite Crosses

Always Christian symbols, these stone crosses come in a variety of shapes: lantern crosses, wheel crosses, four-holed crosses and so on. Crosses had a few uses, but the two main ones were churchyard crosses to demarcate graveyards, and wayside markers. These markers were placed to help walkers travel to church or cross country, and they would mark the safest and easiest route. There are the remains of one on the St Michael's Causeway, essential as the tide turns.

Holy Wells

Mostly pre-Christian, these wells mark naturally occurring springs, many of which are still flowing. These wells are often associated with local folklore and pagan worship, as churches were often built alongside wells in an effort to combine the old and new religions. You may find scraps of coloured ribbons tied to branches around the well. These are known as clooties and act as prayers and offerings. You may also see painted stones and candles. As you can see, these wells are still a place of worship today and you should not take anything from these sites.

Mining

Cornwall's oldest and wealthiest industry has always been mining. The county is incredibly rich in metal and mineral deposits, which have fuelled Cornwall's history. As you walk you will see remnants of the tin, copper and clay mining industries. Beyond these major deposits, Cornwall was also rich in gold, uranium, arsenic, cadmium, lead and zinc. Even today, people are exploring lithium mining.

During the global industrial revolution it was said that at the bottom of a mineshaft anywhere in the world you would find a Cornishman showing the locals how to mine. Due to its geography, the rocks in the soil and the sea that surrounds it, Cornwall was easily the most cosmopolitan area of Britain, with global connections from every mine and port. The Cornish were global exporters of skills, intelligence and commodities.

Padstow

While Padstow originally grew as a fishing village, and it does still have a fishing industry, it is now better known as a tourist attraction and food destination due to Rick Stein's fish restaurant. From opening his restaurant in 1975, Stein's reputation and restaurants grew; he published books and became a well-known TV personality. This connection has earned Padstow the nickname of PadStein. Since then, the town and surrounding coast have become known for offering the best dining in Cornwall, and gradually this effect has rippled out all over Cornwall. I recommend you try the fish!

St Petroc

One of Cornwall's three patron saints, along with St Piran and St Michael. St Petroc is a well-documented figure who was born in Wales in 468 and died in Cornwall in 564. On return from a pilgrimage to Rome he was washed ashore at the mouth of the Camel River at Trebetherick. He founded a monastery and school, which came to be called Petrocs-Stow (Petroc's Place), now Padstow.

St Petroc's Church, Padstow

There has been a church on this site since 518, when it was founded by St Petroc. Vikings burned it to the ground in 981. It was rebuilt in 1100 and replaced in 1425, which is the church you see today. **St Petroc Minor Church** is in a sheltered location. This church was modernised in the nineteenth century then stripped back again. Its exterior architecture is unusual, with more embellishments than is usual on Cornish churches, and the exterior belies the magnificent interior. It is well worth having a look inside.

St Breock Longstone

This is the largest and heaviest monolith in Cornwall, believed to have been erected between 2500 BC and 1500 BC. The stone is five metres tall, three of which are above ground. It is also known as Men Gurta and has featured in local history for centuries, often as a meeting place. As with other prehistoric monoliths its original purpose is unknown, but like all prehistoric structures, the theories include ritual elements.

St Clements Church, Withiel

This church has a long connection with the Vyvyan family. In 1523 a Thomas Vyvyan rebuilt the derelict church to the joy of the local parishioners. Later, one of his descendants was responsible for closing the village pub, The Old Pig and Whistle. Some you win, some you lose.

Lanivet Church

There are lots of things to see here, including an ancient, inscribed stone, circa fifth century, a hogback grave from the tenth century and several Celtic crosses. If you stand beside one particular cross in the middle of the churchyard, you are reputedly standing in the dead centre of Cornwall! If you examine the stone you might see a man with a tail. Or a set of keys hanging from a belt. There's also mediaeval glass in the windows, and bells have rung from the tower since 1538.

St Fimbarrus Church, Fowey

The journey's beginning and end. It is packed with history – keep an eye out in the churchyard for part of the roof finials that fell after a lightning strike. This is the second-tallest church in Cornwall.

Fowey

Home to a very deep river harbour, and offering excellent shelter, Fowey has a long history as a trading settlement. Today it is a busy sailing town but is still home to large tankers and cruise ships. It's always quite a sight when these massive vessels head up the river, towering over the properties on either side.

LANIVET TO FOWEY VIA HELMAN TOR
North to South (Eastern Route)

OS Map: 107

WCs: All facilities at Lanivet & Fowey. Also – The Crown Inn at Lanlivery; The Fishermans Arms, Golant

Length: 13.5 miles

Link: https://cornishwalks.com/gpx-saints/

DIRECTIONS:

0–3 miles: Lanivet to Saints' Split

1. From **Lanivet Church** walk up Rectory Road with the school on your right. Follow the road for nearly a mile until you reach a T-junction and turn right, heading under the bypass. At the next T-junction you have two options.

2. The next section follows the Saints' Way and we refer to it as the Three Crosses section, as you will pass three ancient stone crosses if you take this route. However this is a busy lane with farm machinery and fast traffic. If you wish to avoid this section, cross the road, turn right and take the first left, heading towards Trebell Green, where

you will rejoin the Saints' Way at Step 5. This lane is steep but quiet.

3. To walk the Three Crosses section, turn left at the T-junction and stick close

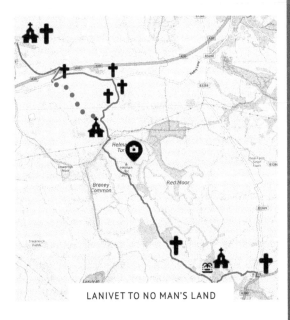

LANIVET TO NO MAN'S LAND

to the hedgerow. Walk just under a mile until the first right-hand turning. Examine the stone cross in the hedgerow then turn up towards Fenton Pitts. This next lane is quiet.

4. Just before the next turning there is another cross in the left-hand hedge. As the lane bends left take the right-hand turning towards Trebell Green. This is a very quiet lane and you will begin to see glimpses of Helman Tor ahead. At a bend in the road you can see another cross in a private garden. Carry on down the lane.

5. Shortly after the cross in the garden, you come to a triangular junction with a Saints' Way finger post in the centre of the green. Take the lower, left-hand lane, and then turn left. This is the road you would have taken if you avoided the Three Crosses section.

6. Now follow this lane for half a mile. At the first left-hand road turning the Saints' Way splits. The left-hand junction is flanked by some large granite stones and crosses a small stream. This is the route for the Saints' Way East, which passes **Helman Tor**.

3–6.5 miles: Saints' Split to No Man's Land

7. Take this turning and walk uphill to a rough car park. It is well worth heading through the car park and up on to the tor, as the views are magnificent. Leaving the car park, follow the Wilderness Trail towards Red Moor, which is half a mile on the signpost. The tarmac road ends and you're now off-road for the first time since Lanivet.

8. Follow this path for a little over a mile. Eventually the path begins to head downhill and the views open up. Ahead you can see the four spires on **Lanlivery Church,** where you are heading. When the path joins the road, turn left and follow the road all the way into Lanlivery.

9. When you get into the village turn right at the T-junction in front of the church. The Crown Inn to your right and the church are both well worth a visit.

If you wish to visit **St Brevita's Holy Well**, follow the footpath on the right just after the pub. Walk a hundred metres and take the metal gate on the left heading into a school field, access is granted. Turn right and follow the path down to a wooden pavilion. Turn left, passing the pavilion and cross a wooden bridge. Now turn right, when the path veers left, take a small little path down to a tiny stream, the holy well is at the end of this path and practically invisible. It's five minutes from the pub but hard to find and there are no signs. Now return to the road.

Continue along the road heading out of the village and then take the left-hand turning. There is a Saints' Way sign on the little triangular piece of ground, but it might be overgrown.

10. Continue downhill, passing a small lane that says 'Unsuitable for Caravans'. Just after a property called Pelyn Tor there's a small flight of steps in the hedgerow on the left. Walk up into the field and follow the path up to the top left-hand corner. You pass a large standing stone in the field, this was erected recently as a birthday present to a previous resident. Climb over a stile and head into the next field. Continue uphill, keeping the hedge on your left.

11. The path now joins a busy road with no pavement. Turn right and walk down towards the A390, facing the oncoming traffic. At the vets, cross the road and pass the collection of cottages at No Man's Land, and another granite cross.

6.5–10.5 miles: No Man's Land to Golant

12. *CAUTION.* You now need to walk a short section along the A390. Looking to your left you can just see at the bottom, on the bend in the road, a small right-hand turning. This is where you are heading for. There is a traffic island here where you can cross over, but the verge is overgrown and you will need to walk on the road. This is a busy and fast road so take lots of care, whichever side of the road you chose to walk down. It is easier to cross here at the island than down near the bend, but you will need to walk on the road on several occasions.

13. At the bend in the road, take the small right-hand turning and follow a small lane heading uphill and away from the A390. As this road bends to the left, follow the Saints' Way signpost and turn right up onto a concrete drive leading into a farmyard. Follow the concrete drive through the farmyard and through two large metal gates. Follow the path

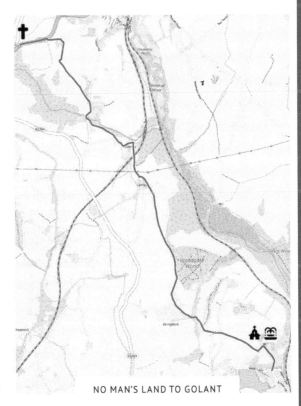

NO MAN'S LAND TO GOLANT

WALKING WITH SAINTS AND TINNERS

down between two hedgerows until the path is blocked by two gates. Take the wooden left-hand gate, which has a footpath symbol.

14. The path eventually joins a small road. Turn right and continue downhill. Follow the road over the small river and take the left-hand turning towards Milltown. When you reach the hamlet of Milltown, turn right after the red postbox in the wall. Continue along the road and head uphill. When the road splits, take the left-hand fork and continue walking uphill for a mile and a half.

15. Walk past the drive to Woodgate and keep an eye out for a stile on the left-hand side, roughly 300 yards after the Woodgate sign. Climb up into the field. It is quite a steep climb to the exit in the top right-hand corner of the field.

16. The path now heads along a field, crosses a small road, enters another field that you cross the middle of, bears right and then crosses a farmer's track and into another field. Here you bear left to exit the field at the far left-hand corner with the church to your left. Leave the field and head along the road towards the church.

10.5–13.5 miles: Golant to Fowey

17. From **St Sampson's Church** follow the road downhill into Golant. Cross over at the crossroads, keeping the Sunday House to your right, and walk along the road. There is a nice little pub, the Fishermans Arms, down to your left if you want to stop for some refreshments on the creek-side. Turn left at the Downs Hill sign and then walk up past a house called Hendre on your left, following the Saints' Way signposts. Keep walking up this little residential lane and eventually it turns into a footpath. Stick to the main path through the woodland, ignoring any left or right spurs as it gradually comes down into a little creek known as Sawmills.

18. At the bottom of the creek cross the small wooden bridge over the stream and then immediately turn right, heading up

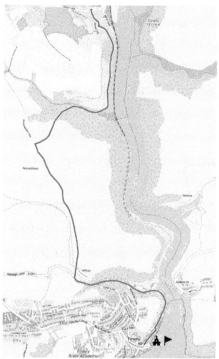

GOLANT TO FOWEY

32

the footpath. Keep to this path heading uphill, then walk out of the woods up into a field and continue along the path. Pass through a wooden kissing-gate towards some agricultural buildings and out onto a concrete drive. At the junction, turn left onto the little road and walk downhill for just under a mile. At the T-junction at the bottom of the road turn left and follow the road into **Fowey**. Although small this road can get busy, so keep to the sides. Follow this road all the way to **St Fimbarrus Church** in the heart of the town and the end of your journey.

God and in Memory of

FOWEY TO LANIVET VIA HELMAN TOR
South to North (Eastern Route)

OS Map: 107

WCs: All facilities at Lanivet & Fowey. Also – The Crown Inn at Lanlivery; The Fishermans Arms, Golant

Length: 13.5 miles

Link: https://cornishwalks.com/gpx-saints/

DIRECTIONS:

0–3 miles: Fowey to Golant
1. From the front of **St Fimbarrus Church** in the town centre, turn left and follow the one-way system out of the town. Walk for a mile until you reach your first right-hand turning towards Penventinue. Walk uphill for just under a mile, and when the road ends take the footpath to your right, behind some agricultural sheds. Follow this path between two fields and down into the woods.

2. As you head into the woods there is a fork; take the left-hand path and walk down the hill. When you get to the creek take the footpath over the stream and continue on the path until you walk into Golant.

3. Follow the road through the village without dropping down to the waterfront. At the crossroads, head straight across

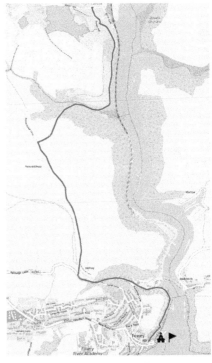

FOWEY TO GOLANT

and walk up the hill towards **St Sampson's Church** at the top. I would describe this hill as obnoxious.

3–7 miles: Golant to No Man's Land

4. Explore the church, re-pack your lungs, then head back on up the road. Just after the bend in the road take the footpath to the right. Cross the wooden stile into the field and keep to the right-hand side. At the second pylon, cut across the field to the granite stile in the hedge. Head across the next field, veering slightly left, and exit via the wooden stile. Cross a

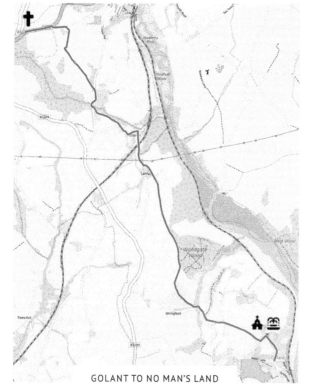

GOLANT TO NO MAN'S LAND

lane and go through a wooden gate then head down to the next field. This field often has horses in it. Continue downhill, heading towards the metal gate in the treeline opposite. Exit via a stile onto a road. Turn right.

5. Stay on the lane for almost two miles until you reach the hamlet of Milltown. Shortly after, walk under a railway bridge and follow the road left. Walk uphill with a small stream to your left until you reach a sign on your left for the Saints' Way. Take this path and head uphill for half a mile, where the path will join a farm track. Pass through the farm via two metal gates and down onto a small road. Turn left and walk down to a busy main road.

6. *CAUTION:* This is a fast and busy section of road. Cross the A390 and walk uphill to the right-hand turning to Bodmin, keeping to the right-hand side of the road. There is a large cross on the green at the junction and a few cottages. This is known as No Man's Land. When you get to some farm gates, cross the road and head up some granite steps and into the field.

7–10.5 miles: No Man's Land to Saints' Split

7. Walk along the field, keeping to the right-hand edge. Exit the field via a wooden gate then head downhill through the next field, following the signs. You pass a large standing stone in the field, this was erected recently as a birthday present to a previous resident. Exit down a flight of steps onto a road. Turn right and walk into Lanlivery; you should be able to see the **Lanlivery Church** ahead.

8. Just before the Crown Inn, you may wish to visit **St Brevita's Holy Well.** Follow the footpath off to the left just before the pub. Walk a hundred metres and take the metal gate on the left heading into a school field, access is granted. Turn right and follow the path down to a wooden pavilion. Turn left, passing the pavilion and cross a wooden bridge. Now turn right, when the path veers left, take a small little path down to a tiny stream, the holy well is at the end of this path and practically invisible. It's five minutes from the pub but hard to find and there are no signs. Now return to the road.

From the church, take the road out of the village towards Luxulyan. At the crossroads ignore the sign to Luxulyan and now follow the sign to Lanivet. After a third of a mile, keep an eye out for a right-hand turning to an unmade lane. It will be signposted for the Saints' Way. Stay on this footpath. Sometimes it can be waterlogged, but you can avoid the worst section by taking a small gate to the left and walking along the right-hand side of the hedge until you get to a second gate where you can rejoin the track.

9. When you reach the car park for **Helman Tor**, the path becomes a small lane. It is well worth heading up the tor to enjoy the view before returning to the lane and walking downhill. When you reach a T-junction turn right: this is the junction where the east and west paths meet.

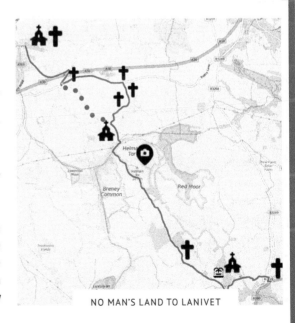

NO MAN'S LAND TO LANIVET

10.5–13.5 miles: Saints' Split to Lanivet

10. Now walk for half a mile until you reach a right-hand turning at a small triangular green.

Detour: If you are looking for a shortcut, wish to avoid a fast lane or are not concerned about the three stone crosses, stay on this road for another mile until you reach a T-junction. Turn right and then left to rejoin the Saints' Way. At that junction keep your eyes peeled for a stone cross and two stone route markers. This lane is very quiet with lovely views when you reach the summit.

11. At the green, take the right-hand turning and follow the lane uphill. As you pass a few houses, look into the last garden on the left to see a stone cross.

Follow the road as it bends right and walk to the T-junction, then turn left. Just after the junction there is another stone cross tucked into the hedge on your right. Keep walking until the next T-junction, where there is another cross in the hedge directly across the road.

12. Turn left. This road, though minor, can be busy with fast traffic. Take care for the next half mile until the right-hand turning to Lanivet. This is a junction of a few lanes, and there are some interesting stone markers as well as another cross at the left-hand junction a few yards ahead.

13. Having explored, take the road down to Lanivet. Head through the underpass then take the left-hand turning and walk down to **Lanivet Church**, where this section of the walk ends.

THE SAINTS' WAY (EASTERN ROUTE): POINTS OF INTEREST

Helman Tor

A stunning granite outcrop within several nature reserves. This is a perfect spot for a picnic, and if you have time it's worth exploring some of the nearby reserves. There is also a cross carved into one of the rock tops.

St Brevita's Church, Lanlivery

Sitting on a small hilltop, the church tower can be seen from miles away. The tower is 100 feet tall and capped with four distinctive pinnacles. It was added in the seventeenth century, making St Brevita the third-tallest church in Cornwall. It was once painted white as a landmark to sailors; however, given how far inland it is, a rainy day might have obscured visibility. Happily, it's always sunny in Cornwall! There is an excellent wagon ceiling in the nave and a Norman coffin in the graveyard. Early records suggest the church was dedicated to St Vorck but was later replaced by St Brevita; **St Brevita's Holy Well** is nearby. To see it you need to walk past the Crown Inn. And as you're passing it would be rude not to call in.

St Sampson's Church, Golant

A church wrapped up in the Arthurian legend of Tristan and Iseult. All the land around here has links to the legend, including Tristan's fight with King Marc down on the shore of the Fowey and Marc's possible home at Castel Dore. Saint Sampson himself was famed for freeing the local villagers of a dragon that had been plaguing them, and if you look around the church you will see images of dragons all around.

There is also a holy well just by the entrance to the church.

Saint Sampson

Saint Sampson was born in Wales circa 485. In 521, as a bishop, he decided to go on a pilgrimage to Cornwall. It is believed that he lived in a cave overlooking the River Fowey, below where the church now stands. The cave had previously been the home of a dragon that was terrorising the villagers and, seeing their plight, Sampson slew it for them. As he had rid the village of this dragon, the parishioners built a church in his name in thanks. The alternative is that Sampson felt the village needed a monastic settlement and built one himself.

If you go into the church, see if you can find the dragon carved into the end of one of the wooden benches, or in the stained-glass windows. To the left of the church porch is an old holy well. It is said that Saint Sampson, faint from fasting one day, prayed for water and a spring arose. It is more likely, though, that this well predates the church, as many churches were built near or on the sites of existing places of worship. Springs and wells have been sites of ancient Cornish worship all across the county.

Tristan and Iseult

The love story of Tristan and Iseult has been performed over the centuries, the most notable examples being Wagner's opera *Tristan and Isolde* or the Kneehigh Theatre's production of *Tristan and Yseult*. There are many variations of the tale and all are complicated, but the bare bones are that Tristan is sent by his Uncle Mark, King of the Cornish, to escort Mark's new bride, Iseult, from Ireland. On the journey home, Tristan and Iseult accidentally drink the love potion destined for Mark and they fall in love. Iseult marries the king but remains in love with Tristan, and they continue to see each other.

After her marriage to King Mark, Iseult gave a cloak to the church, in thanks for blessing her marriage. The lovers' gate at the front of the church is said to mark the spot where Iseult stood and looked out for Tristan. Trees currently block the view of the river, but there are spots in the graveyard where you can overlook the river and imagine Iseult standing in the wind, her marriage cloak blowing about her as she watches to see if her lover is returning. Ultimately, they are discovered, and Mark is furious. Whichever variation you follow it is the basic love triangle and most of the protagonists die in tragic circumstances.

LANIVET TO FOWEY VIA TYWARDREATH
North to South (Western Route)

OS Map: 107

WCs: All facilities at Lanivet & Fowey – In between various facilities at Par, Tywardreath & Luxulyan

Length: 15 miles

Link: https://cornishwalks.com/gpx-saints/

DIRECTIONS:

0–3 miles: Lanivet to Saints' Split

1. From **Lanivet Church** walk up Rectory Road with the school on your right. Follow the road for nearly a mile until you reach a T-junction. Turn right, heading under the bypass. At the next T-junction you have two options.

2. The next section follows the Saints' Way and we refer to it as the Three Crosses section, as you will pass three ancient stone crosses if you take this route. However this is a busy lane with farm machinery and fast traffic. If you wish to avoid this section, cross the road, turn right and take the first left, heading towards Trebell Green, where you will rejoin the Saints' Way at Step 5. This lane is steep but quiet.

3. To walk the Saints' Way turn left at the T-junction and stick close to the hedgerow. Walk just under a mile until

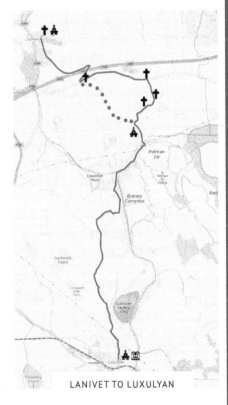

LANIVET TO LUXULYAN

the first right-hand turning. Examine the stone cross in the hedgerow then turn up towards Fenton Pitts. This lane is quiet.

4. Just before the next turning there is another cross in the left-hand hedge. As the lane bends left take the right-hand turning towards Trebell Green. This is a very quiet lane and you will begin to see glimpses of Helman Tor ahead. At a bend in the road you can see another cross in a private garden. Carry on down the lane.

5. Shortly after the cross in the garden, you come to a triangular junction with a Saints' Way finger post in the centre of the green. Take the lower, left-hand lane and then turn left. This is the road you would have taken if you had avoided the Three Crosses section.

6. Now follow this lane for half a mile. At the first left-hand road turning the Saints' Way splits. The left-hand junction is flanked by some large granite stones and crosses a small stream. This is the route for the Saints' Way East, which passes Helman Tor.

3–6 miles: Saints' Split to Luxulyan

7. Helman Tor is well worth visiting, otherwise ignore the turning, and continue on the lane. The vegetation to the left and right of the road is very swamp-like and it's easy to imagine creatures tracking you in the undergrowth. In reality the most exciting thing you are likely to see is a butterfly.

8. Stay on the road until you reach the hamlet of Gunwen then turn left, passing the **Gunwen Methodist Chapel** on your right. Walk out of the hamlet and take the first right-hand turning. The Saints' Way signpost might be hidden under the vegetation but there is also a blue 'Unsuitable for HGV' sign that is easier to spot.

9. Head uphill and follow the road passing Corgee Farm, then further on, just after Tredinnick Barn, take the small unmade road to your left. The next mile will be off-road.

10. Follow the driveway until you get to a lawned area and turn right towards a small wooden gate. On the skyline you can see a conical clay tip that sits above St Austell. Enter the field and take the path heading left and downhill.

11. Exit the field at a small wooden gate in the bottom corner of the field. In the next field, follow the path along the bottom until it heads into the trees. The turning into the trees is adjacent to two large granite boulders in the field.

12. This is an ancient footpath that runs through a swampish area with lots of boardwalks. At the end of this section, climb the wooden stile into a field full

of boulders, and sometimes cows. Walk uphill towards the pylon, keeping the hedgerow of trees to your left. If there are cows and you wish to avoid them, walk on the other side of the trees heading in the same direction. Pass the pylon and leave the field over a wooden and granite stile in the top left corner.

13. Cross the small road and cut across a patch of grass and down onto another road. Turn right. You are now walking into the village of Luxulyan. When the road bends to the right, take the left-hand junction, passing Atwell Farm Park, and continue towards **St Julian's Church**.

6–9 miles: Luxulyan to St Blazey

There are three detours in this section. Read ahead to see what you want to do.

Full Detour 1: Avoiding cows: alternate route avoiding cattle. 2 miles, all road

On the next section you are likely to encounter cattle. If you wish to avoid them follow this detour. Head downhill past the post office. Walk out of the village and at the bottom of the hill take the right-hand

turning to the Luxulyan Valley. Walk for just under two miles, then at a car park veer right and continue under the **Treffry Viaduct**. At the next T-junction follow the directions from Step 22.

Tiny Detour 2: Visiting Holy Well

When you get to the church and the T-junction, turn left and head down the road towards the post office. To visit the holy well of St Cyors head past the post office and, just after the churchyard on the left-hand side, walk down a few steps leading off the road. Explore the holy well then return to the Saints' Way.

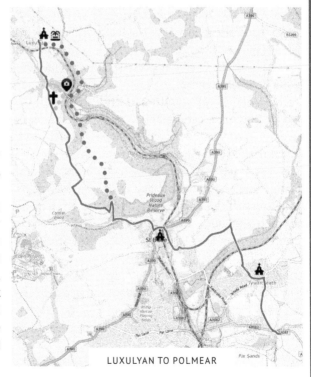

LUXULYAN TO POLMEAR

14. From the church head towards the post office. Turn right just before the post office and follow the Saints' Way markers. The residential lane ends at a railway bridge. Cross the bridge then climb over a granite stile and into a field. For the next two miles you are likely to encounter cattle.

15. Head straight across the field, making for the gap in the trees on the other side. Cross into the next field and cross it towards a large granite stile. You are now on rough moorland. Follow the path into the trees: the next section can be boggy. Follow the yellow markers until you get to a wooden stile. Climb over and take the two small bridges across a stream and a leat. Just after the leat the path splits.

Detour 3: Recommended

The next detour takes in the **Treffry Viaduct**. The route can be boggy and there are abandoned industrial works, so dogs need to be on lead and children supervised. If you don't want to explore, ignore the left-hand turning and walk uphill, crossing the next two fields on the right-hand edge, then follow the instructions from Step 16.

Otherwise, take the left-hand turning. Keep a close eye on children and dogs. After a few metres there is another left-hand turning just after a sluice gate.

Upper Path. The better option if the path is very wet. Walk straight ahead and stay on this track until you reach some granite steps. Take the steps up to the small gate then turn left and follow the path for about a hundred metres through the bracken and down to another wooden gate. Head down the wooden steps and explore the viaduct. If you have a problem with heights maybe avoid walking too far over the viaduct – and don't look over the side! You're 27 metres up. Return to the wooden steps and back up onto the scrubland.

Lower Path. At the sluice gate turn left and head towards the stream. Just before an underpass, scramble up the rocks onto the path above then turn right. This path is very atmospheric and is littered with industrial archaeology. As you get closer to the viaduct the empty leat to your left will become more obvious. This leat was designed to flow through the viaduct itself, under the granite slabs. As you arrive at the viaduct look to your right, where there should be a flight of wooden steps. Explore the viaduct and then come back to the steps. Head up the steps, through a small gate and onto the scrubland.

Upper and Lower Paths rejoined. You now need to head to the top left of this very large field. Leave the field via a series of three stiles: two wooden, one granite.

16. You are now back on the Saints' Way. Follow the right-hand hedge down to a small wooden gate, a stile, then another gate. In the next field head uphill, cutting directly across the field towards a metal gate. Keep to the right-hand side of the next field and go through another metal gate.

17. You now need to navigate around the farm barns, making sure you are on the other side of the electric fence. Use the plastic collars on the fence to unlatch it and replace it. There are a few access points along the way if you need to avoid cattle. Keep to the right-hand side of the field and as you pass the farm buildings you should see a wooden stile in the hedgerow ahead.

18. Climb over the stile and head into the woods, following the path. Keep your eyes peeled for evidence of abandoned mining features, such as sluices and leats.

19. At the wooden kissing-gate enter the field and walk directly ahead, uphill across the field. When you get to the trees on the horizon, climb over the granite stile. Cross the small lane and walk down the concrete drive, following it around to the right.

20. The lane is blocked by two metal gates as you walk through the farmyard. Remember to close these gates behind you. After the second gate head uphill

and at the brow take the wooden stile to your left into a field. Keep to the left-hand side and head down the field. You are now looking out over St Austell Bay. There is an Iron Age hillfort in the field to your left but there is no right of access, and you will need to obtain permission to visit.

21. Leave the field via a wooden stile in the left-hand hedgerow. There are no more cattle on this walk. Take the path along the wooded edge until you get to a stile. Along the way you might spot the Gribbin Daymark on the horizon. We are heading towards it. Climb over the stile and head right along the path as it starts to zigzag all the way down through the wooded valley. At the bottom of the hill, cross a small stream and then join the road and turn right.

22. At the bottom of this lane turn left at the T-junction and follow it all the way down to the junction with the A390 at St Blazey. Turn left.

9–11 miles: St Blazey to Polmear
23. Walk past the petrol station and just after the level crossing take the right-hand turning to Kilhallon. This is a slight detour from the Saints' Way, but it's quicker and we don't miss anything. There is no pavement so keep an eye out for traffic. Head uphill, then pass through the hamlet of Kilhallon and continue on the road. At the crossroads, head over in the direction of Lanescot.

Walk for a further half mile and then take the unmade lane on the right heading downhill just after Marsh Hill House. Follow the path downhill over a stream then straight ahead and uphill under a railway bridge.

24. At the top of the path turn right, walk towards the houses and take the left-hand road. This is **Tywardreath**. At the junction with North Street bear right then immediately left down Church Street. Follow the road past **St Andrew's Church** and then turn right in front of the New Inn. Follow the road for half a mile, out of the village and down to Polmear by Par Beach.

11–12.5 miles: Polmear to Tregaminion

25. Cross the main road, walk under the flyover and head towards the Ship Inn. Take the unmade road to the left of the pub and follow the Saints' Way sign uphill past the houses. At the junction do not join the coast path but turn left into a field. Head uphill, and as you climb be sure to look behind you as the views are excellent and you may be grateful for the rest. Cross a small private lane and continue uphill in the next field, heading to the top left-hand corner.

26. Exit the field and take the path down to the main road. This is a fast road and for a short section it is without a footpath, so take care. Cross the road and turn right. After a few yards join the footpath and continue walking uphill until you reach the right-hand turning to Polkerris and Menabilly. Cross the road again and head towards Menabilly. Stay on this road until you get to **Tregaminion Church** on your left-hand side.

Detour: If you want to extend your walk you can take the next section along the coast path. Shortly before you get to Tregaminion

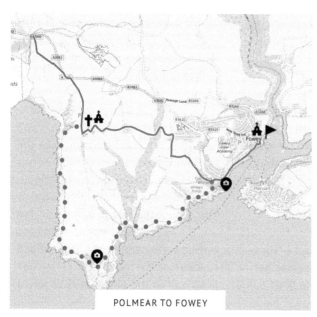

POLMEAR TO FOWEY

Church there is a right-hand path across a field, towards the trees. You will then meet the coast path. Turn left and stay on the coast path for the next four miles until you reach Readymoney Cove, then follow the directions from Step 29. This adds an additional two miles to your walk. This section of coast path takes us through Daphne du Maurier country, the location of many of her novels including *Rebecca*. You also pass the Gribbin Daymark. This section has glorious views and small beaches to stop at for a swim.

12.5–15 miles:
Tregaminion to Fowey

27. Take the lane beside the church and head down towards the farmyard, where the path cuts directly through the farm. Follow the signs carefully and keep any dogs close by. Take the path out of the yard, across a field and over a rickety wooden bridge. The path continues for a mile through various fields until you arrive in the hamlet of Lankelly.

28. Turn right when you reach the road and walk until you reach Rashleigh Lane. Turn left down the road. Halfway down, take the right-hand footpath signposted for the Saints' Way. Follow this footpath down through the woods to Readymoney Cove.

29. From the cove follow the road towards **Fowey**. Ignore all left-hand turns and enjoy the views over the Fowey Estuary. Once in the village make your way to **St Fimbarrus Church** and enjoy a well-deserved rest.

FOWEY TO LANIVET VIA TYWARDREATH
South to North (Western Route)

OS Map: 107

WCs: All facilities at Lanivet & Fowey – In between various facilities at Par, Tywardreath & Luxulyan

Length: 15 miles

Link: https://cornishwalks.com/gpx-saints/

DIRECTIONS:

0–2.5 miles: Fowey to Tregaminion

1. Starting from the road in front of **St Fimbarrus Church**, walk right, against the traffic, and head towards Readymoney Cove via Esplanade. Turn left onto Esplanade opposite a freestanding red postbox. When you get to Readymoney Cove, take the footpath at the far end of the cove. It is clearly marked for the Saints' Way.

2. Head uphill, following the signposts to Tregaminion. When the path splits take the left-hand junction. The path now pops out onto a quiet tarmac road: turn left and continue uphill.

At the T-junction with Coombe Lane, turn right. This road can be a little busier. The road finally turns downhill a bit as you walk into the hamlet of Lankelly. Walk past the right-hand turn and after

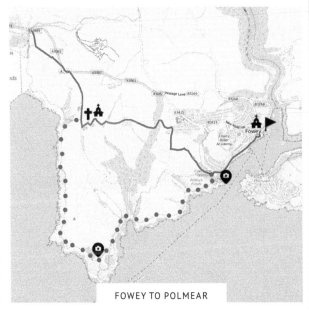

FOWEY TO POLMEAR

55

about ten metres, on the left-hand side, the Saints' Way continues as a footpath, which runs down the left-hand side of a large hedge. Walk through a small gate and follow the path downhill.

3. Follow this path to Tregaminion for a mile. Head through a kissing-gate and under a low stone bridge then follow the path uphill and over a sheep stile. As you walk along, look over to your left and in the distance you should see a red and white tower; this is the Gribbin Daymark. The path crosses a private drive and then continues, having first climbed over another sheep stile. The path runs between two fields and ends at a small

gate and a long flight of steps. At the bottom, take the small wooden bridge over the stream and continue until the path brings you into a farmyard.

4. The Saints' Way walks right through the centre of this working farm, so be prepared to wait if the farmer is moving any stock, and keep an eye out for tractors. As you reach the barns turn right and then follow the drive left uphill and out onto the road.

2.5–6 miles: Tregaminion to St Blazey

5. With **Tregaminion Church** to your left, turn right at the T-junction and walk ahead until you meet the main road. This is a busy road so cross it with care. Follow the pavement downhill, until it ends. The footpath continues about twenty feet downhill on the other side of the road – its entrance is concealed in the hedges. Cross with care and then head over the stone stile and then directly after it a wooden one.

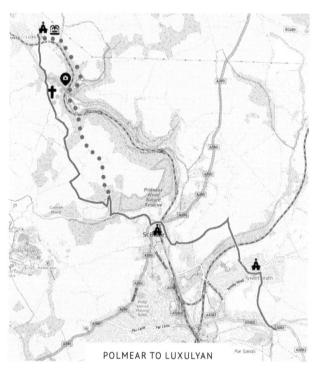

POLMEAR TO LUXULYAN

6. The path now cuts straight across the field. As you reach the brow of the hill you can see Par Sands beach and a holiday park below. Ahead of you, on the horizon, are the clay tips of Mid Cornwall. When you get to a small drive look out for the granite stile leading into the next field. Now walk downhill, and gradually the lake in front of the holiday cabins will come into view. Walk to the right-hand side of the lake and ignore all tempting gates to your left. As you walk down through the field you may spot the path in the grass, but keep heading towards the hedge with the lake just to your left. When you reach the far side of the field, head through the large gap in the hedge and walk down the path. The path joins a small private lane and then comes out onto the main road.

7. Stay on this side of the road and walk under the flyover, then take the second turning right heading up to **Tywardreath**. Follow the road into the heart of the village, at the T-junction, turn left. Continue along Church Street. Just as you pass **St Andrew's Church** the road bends to the right, follow the road uphill passing the village hall on your right. At the junction of a few small roads cross over and walk up Wood Lane.

8. At the end of Wood Lane turn right towards the Saints' Way footpath sign. Follow the footpath down under the railway line and into a swampy area.

Take the bridge over the stream and walk uphill. When the path joins a road turn left.

9. Stay on the road for a mile, ignoring any turnings and pass through the hamlet of Kilhallon. Follow the road down to the A390 watching out for any traffic. At the main road turn left, pass the garage and then cross over and take the turning to Luxulyan via Prideaux Road.

6–9 miles: St Blazey to Luxulyan

10. Head up Prideaux Road for half a mile then take the right-hand turning to Luxulyan Valley. Walk uphill until you get to a metal gate and wooden kissing-gate on your left.

Detour: The next section heads through farmland and it is likely you will encounter cattle. You can avoid this by staying on the road for two miles following the signs for Luxulyan. Just after the **Treffry Viaduct**, take the left-hand fork in the road and continue until you reach a T-junction. Turn left and head up towards **Luxulyan Church**. There is a holy well to St Cyors just before the churchyard. Take the stone steps on the right-hand side heading down to the well.

11. To stay on the Saints' Way, head through the wooden gate and into the woods, where the footpath zigzags up through the trees. At the top of the woods turn left, head over the stile and follow the path. At the end of the track climb up granite steps, through the kissing-gate and into a large field. Turn right and head uphill. At the top of the field either go through the open gate or over the wooden stile. Head onto the lane and turn right towards the farm buildings.

12. Follow the concrete lane through two large farm gates and then follow the drive as it veers left up to a small road. Walk directly across the road and over the stile opposite into a field. Head towards the trees, veering very slightly right and through a wooden gate in the treeline. The path heads through the trees until it ends at a wooden stile to the right. Climb into the field and walk towards the farm buildings, staying to the left of the field. There is likely to be cattle in this field.

13. The path skirts around the farm buildings but is well signed. Having passed the barns, go through a large five-bar gate and head directly across the field, walking downhill towards a small wooden gate, a granite stile and then through another small wooden gate. Climb the next field and cross a set of three stiles.

Detour: To avoid the viaduct, cross the next two fields, sticking to the left-hand side. Resume the directions at Step 14. Dogs and children will need to be closely supervised around the viaduct and through the woods.

To visit **Treffry Viaduct**, cross this large field on its diagonal. Your exit is in the bottom right. You won't see it for a while as it's hidden in the treeline. Take any route across the field and follow any path through the bracken until you are at the far corner.

There are two exits quite close to each other. Head to the one on the right, where the path leads downhill towards a small wooden gate and a flight of wooden steps. Directly in front of you is the mouth of the viaduct.

Having explored the viaduct, you have a choice of two paths to return to the Saints' Way, both of which pass through sections of overgrown industrial heritage.

Upper Path. This is great if the lower path is waterlogged. Head back up the flight of wooden steps, walk back through the bracken and turn right to exit via a second gate and down a few granite steps. Follow the path until you intersect with the Saints' Way. Turn right at the finger post. You are now back on the Saints' Way.

Lower Path. This route is more interesting, but it has a few turns, isn't signposted and can get waterlogged. With the viaduct at your back, take the footpath into the trees. Stay on the path until you spot a rough path down to your left, running below the path you are walking on. Scramble down on the left-hand side and take the lower path with the stream on your right. Walk upstream until you intersect with the Saints' Way, then turn right at the finger post. You are now back on the Saints' Way.

14. Now follow the path over a leat, then a stream, then over a stile. This section can be boggy but it is well marked. Follow the finger posts into an area of scrubland and towards a large stile. Climb over. There may be cattle in the next two fields. Cross diagonally, heading uphill in the direction of the church tower with its distinctive crow's nest.

15. Leave the field via a metal gate and follow the signs towards Luxulyan Church. You are now in Luxulyan. As you join the main road, there is a holy well off to the right. Walk down the road and take the steps down on the left. Then return to the road and walk up to the church.

9–12 miles: Luxulyan to Saints' Split

16. Turn right at the church and head down until just before a T-junction. Cross the small green verge. Cross the road and take the stile up into a field with a pylon in it. Stick to the scrubby tree hedge on your right and make your way to the bottom right corner then take the stile into the woods. Follow the path across various boardwalks as you wander through this swamp. This area has a peaceful and ancient air about it. As you leave this section head up into a fallow field and turn left, following the lower edge of

the field towards a small wooden gate.

17. In the next field walk all the way across to the far top right-hand corner. Exit via a small gate and turn left along a private drive. At the road, turn right and walk for a mile. The rest of the Saints' Way will be on small roads. At the T-junction turn left. At **Gunwen Methodist Chapel** bear right towards **Helman Tor**. Walk for half a mile until you reach a small right-hand lane. This point is where the two Saints' Ways rejoin, east and west.

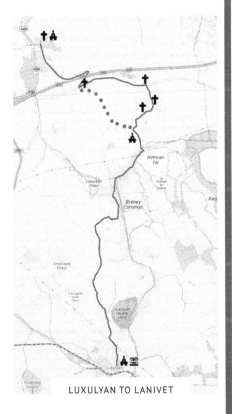

LUXULYAN TO LANIVET

12–15 miles: Saints' Split to Lanivet

18. Walk past the turning and walk for half a mile until you reach a right-hand turning at a small triangular green.

Detour: If you are looking for a shortcut, wish to avoid a fast lane or are not concerned about the three stone crosses, stay on this road for another mile until you reach a T-junction. Turn right and then left to rejoin the Saints' Way. At that junction keep your eyes peeled for a stone cross and two stone route markers. This lane is very quiet with lovely views when you reach the summit.

19. At the green, take the right-hand turning and follow the lane uphill. As you pass a few houses, look into the last garden on the left to see a cross in the garden. Follow the road as it bends right until you reach the T-junction, then turn left. Just after the junction there is another stone tucked into the hedge on your right. Keep walking until the next T-junction, where there is another cross in the hedge directly across the road.

20. Turn left. This road, though minor, can be busy with fast traffic. Take care for the next half mile until the right-hand turning to Lanivet. This is a junction of a few lanes and there are some interesting stone markers, as well as another cross at the left-hand junction a few yards ahead.

21. Having explored, take the road down to Lanivet. Head through the underpass then take the left-hand turning and walk down to **Lanivet Church**, where this section of the walk ends.

THE SAINTS' WAY (WESTERN ROUTE): POINTS OF INTEREST

Gunwen Chapel

An isolated Methodist chapel, this sits in a very tranquil location. It was built in 1869 on the site of a smaller chapel. Across from the chapel runs a little stream hidden in the trees.

St Cyriacus & St Julitta Church, Luxulyan

You will spot the distinctive crow's nest on the tower from some distance as you walk towards the church. It was originally dedicated to St Sulien – the village takes its name from the saint – but the church was rededicated to Cyriacus and Julitta for reasons unknown.

Just down the lane from the church is a holy well dedicated to St Sulien.

Treffry Viaduct

Built by Richard Treffry in 1839, this viaduct is an engineering masterpiece. It has ten arches, spanning 200 metres, and stands 27 metres tall. The viaduct had a dual purpose; it was built to provide a tramway across the valley but also to provide power to the waterwheel. Within the viaduct runs the Carmears Leat, and you can sometimes see the water flowing beneath your feet. A leat is a small man-made water course. The viaduct is a stunning piece of architecture and is now a scheduled monument.

St Andrew's Church, Tywardreath

First dedicated in 1343, this church was heavily rebuilt in 1880. Tywardreath grew as a settlement from the nearby Benedictine monastery that is now lost. It is believed to be in one of the nearby farm fields, but there hasn't been an archaeological dig.

Tywardreath

Tywardreath was home to an important priory, from 1088 to its dissolution in 1536, which was rich, powerful and influential. In its day it stood on the banks of a tidal river; as recently as the late 1700s the tide still reached as far as the village church, but the river gradually silted up. Tywardreath means The House on the Strand, *strand* being an old Saxon word for beach or riverbank. Gradually, over time, through the loss of the priory and its influence and the loss of the river as a trading port, Tywardreath has become the quiet village it is today. Walking through it, though, there is plenty of architectural evidence of its former greatness. The only thing that is missing is the known location of the priory itself, although the best guess places it on the site of Newhouse Farm.

Tregaminion Church

Tregaminion Church was begun in 1813 by William Rashleigh; it is now a Chapel of Ease and is rarely open. In its grounds stand two wayside crosses that would have once acted as route markers. Just as we follow the finger posts today, these crosses provided markers for ancient traders and pilgrims. However, these two crosses were moved here from other discovered locations.

ST MICHAEL'S WAY

This is a very quiet walk that explores the Cornish hinterland, walking through myths and legends. It's also great for spotting wildlife, especially birds.

St Michael's Way can be walked in its entirety in a day. You can return to your starting point via train, bus or taxi. The Penzance train station is two miles down the beach from Marazion. Because of the limited facilities at Lelant I like to start at the end, finishing the walk where there are plenty of facilities and transport options. Added to which, walking towards St Michael's Mount is pretty impressive.

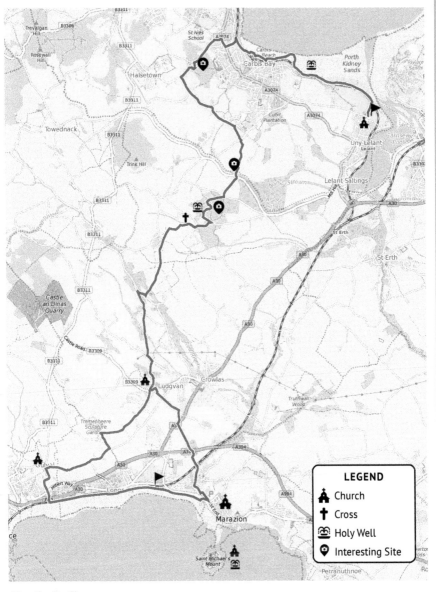

Elevation Profile

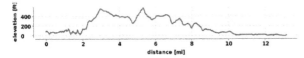

LEGEND

⛪ Church

✝ Cross

♨ Holy Well

◉ Interesting Site

LELANT TO MARAZION / ST MICHAEL'S MOUNT

OS Map: 102

WCs: All facilities at Marazion. Partial facilities at Lelant, Carbis Bay & Ludgvan

Length: 10 or 12.5 miles, depending on southern route

Link: https://cornishwalks.com/gpx-saints/

DIRECTIONS:

The walk begins in front of **St Uny Church**, where there is a large noticeboard describing the path. The whole path is clearly laid out and at all times you will be following the sign of the scallop shell. This section of the path is also the South West Coast Path. The graveyard overlooks the sands, and a golf course runs alongside the path.

0–3 miles: Lelant to Knill's Monument

1. Take the footpath from the church paying attention to the fact that you will be cutting across a golf course. When the path passes under the railway bridge, head left. The path now heads through the dunes and on towards Carbis Bay. Along this section the path passes St Uny's Holy Well. The route to the well is steep, slippery, hard to find and on the cliffside, so I don't describe it here.

2. Eventually the track leaves the dunes and heads into small trees as it skirts behind houses. Walk past Carbis Bay and up onto the main road. Follow the road down towards the Carbis Bay Hotel. The path cuts through the middle of the hotel grounds but is clearly marked. Follow the path out of the hotel and then cross over the railway line. Carry on along the path until you reach a sharp left-hand turn heading uphill. It is marked with the scallop shell and points towards 'Knill's Monument 1 Mile'.

3. Take this footpath uphill until it joins a main road. Turn right and walk down to the Cornish Arms pub. Cross the road and turn left into Tregenna Road and immediately left again onto Steeple Lane. Take this road up to **Knill's Monument**. This is a steep climb but the views at the top are spectacular.

3–5.5 miles: Knill's Monument to Trencrom Hill

4. From Knill's Monument, follow the footpath down through the moorland until it joins the corner of a road. Turn left. Follow the road for three quarters

67

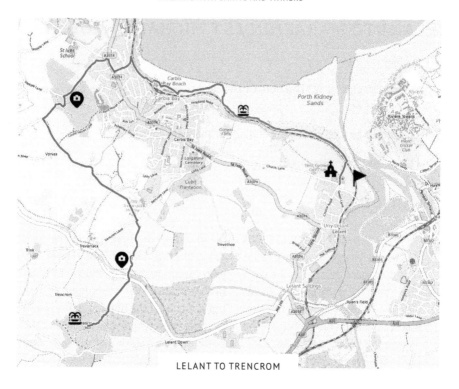

LELANT TO TRENCROM

of a mile until, shortly after a sharp left turn in the road, the path leaves the road. Keep your eyes peeled on the right-hand hedgerow and take the granite steps up off the road. Follow the path through a development then straight over another granite stone stile and out into a big field.

5. As you look across the field you can see some corrugated barns. Head in a diagonal direction across the middle of the field with the corrugated barns to your right. The wooden stile is just to the left of them. Climb into the yard and then head out to the road.

6. Cross the road and take the granite steps up into a field, keeping to the left-hand side, and after a short distance leave the field through a gap in the hedge. Turn right and walk along a wide grass path between the field and an equestrian centre. Keep an eye out for a granite and wooden stile, which is marked for the St Michael's Way.

7. The footpath takes you past a small cottage and down a private lane, and eventually you come to a main road. To your right, in a small meadow, you will see **Bowl Rock**. Now cross the road,

veering left towards the grass verge. Take the footpath up beyond the chapel and turn right heading towards a large field.

8. The path now rises steeply up towards **Trencrom Hill**. Climb this field, keeping to the left-hand side of the hedge. Exit the field via a granite stile at the top left. Cross the road and climb over the granite stile.

9. From this point there are two options.

Route 1. To climb up Trencrom Hill take any of the small paths towards the summit. Having enjoyed the stunning views over the north and south coasts, take any path downhill until you reach an unmade lane. Turn left and follow the lane until you reach a National Trust car park.

Route 2. To avoid the hill, take the path to your left and stay on the path as it circumnavigates the hill and ends at a National Trust car park.

5.5–8.5 miles: Trencrom Hill to Ludgvan

10. From the car park head onto the road and turn right. Walk until the first left-hand turning. Turn left and walk down to a small hamlet, taking the footpath in front of a row of cottages. Follow the small stream and then cross the stile. This section can be wet.

11. The path now continues across nine fields. **Field 1:** head across the field on the left-hand diagonal towards a broken gate just below the telegraph pole. **Field 2:** walk uphill on a left-hand diagonal and exit via a wooden gate. There is a post in the hedgerow signifying its location. **Field 3:** head across the field, veering slightly right towards the wooden gate and exit. **Field 4:** walk directly across field towards a wooden gate and telegraph pole; exit via gate. **Field 5:** cross the field on a right-hand diagonal, heading towards wooden and metal gates. Exit via wooden gate. **Field 6:** walk directly across the field towards the wooden gate just to the right of a telegraph pole. Exit via gate, cross a small footpath and go through the next wooden gate. **Field 7:** walk across the field on a right-hand tangent towards the wooden gate and exit. Cross a farm lane and head through the next wooden gate. **Field 8:** walk on a slight right-hand diagonal towards the wooden gate. As you walk through this field you get glimpses of Ludgvan Church. Don't be fooled into thinking you are nearly there. There are several folds in the land between here and there. Which is a nice way to say the next section is a bit of a rollercoaster. Exit via gate. **Field 9:** keep to the left-hand side of this field and head downhill. You should now be getting good views of St Michael's Mount, depending on how good visibility is. Exit via a wooden stile at the bottom left of the field.

12. The footpath through the trees is short and steep and can be slippery. At

the bottom, join the drive and walk down towards the road. At the road turn right, cross the ford and continue along the road until you meet a junction. Take the left-hand turning and start walking uphill.

13. Shortly after Boskennal Farm take the footpath on the right, via a wooden stile. Keep to the right-hand side of the field. As you enter the next field you need to walk downhill on a right-hand diagonal towards the trees, keeping the pylon

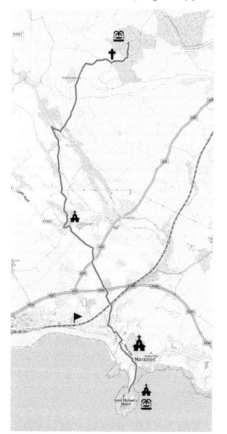

and the church tower directly ahead of you and ignoring the obvious gap in the hedge to your left. Exit via a wooden stile.

14. Cross a small stream and take the track left as it heads through a small, wooded area. Exit via a stile and head uphill through the field towards the pylon. At the top of the field exit via the left of two exits, heading over some granite steps and into the next field. Keep to the right-hand side of this field and exit via the top-right corner through a hole in the hedge.

15. You can now see the church directly ahead of you. Do not be fooled for one second into thinking that the hills are behind you, you've got one more to go.

As the path joins the road, turn left and head downhill. Just after the '30 mph' sign take the footpath on your right and follow the path downhill. At the bottom, cross another little stream and then take the track heading uphill, bearing left. At the top of the hill the path comes out at **Lugdvan Church**. There's a good pub just round the corner if you want a break.

From here the path splits. The eastern route is more direct but crosses a very busy road. The western route passes through Gulval and along the coast path. If you are collecting the pilgrim stamps you need to take the western route.

TRENCROM TO MARAZION (EAST)

EASTERN ROUTE

8.5–10 miles: Ludgvan to Marazion

16a.　From the front of the church, turn left along the road and head towards the White Hart pub. Just after the pub, on the opposite side of the road, is a signpost for the St Michael's Way. Follow the path down through the fields, crossing a small lane as you go. When you reach the next road turn right. There is no footpath and the road can be busy. Follow the road towards a very busy T-junction then head up onto the grass verge to your right and walk over to the traffic island. Cross the road, turn right and then almost immediately take the left-hand stile into a field. Keep to the left of the three fields and exit at the bottom left.

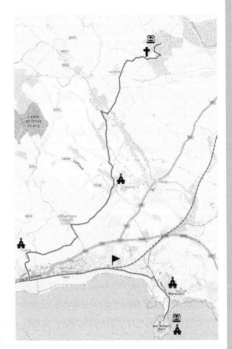

TRENCROM TO MARAZION (WEST)

17a.　At the bottom of the trees the path comes out onto a fast, busy main road. There is no traffic island. Cross with care and head straight onto the footpath ahead and away from the road. Follow the footpath through the Marazion marshes. At one point you will cross the main London train line. There are no barriers, so take care. As you arrive in Marazion, leave the footpath via a granite stile and head up onto a small road. Turn left, crossing a stone bridge, and then head towards the beach.

18a.　From here you can make your way to **St Michael's Mount** – either by boat (there is a fee) or causeway, depending on the tide – or you can return to your car. This is the end of the walk.

WESTERN ROUTE

8.5–12.5 miles: Ludgvan to Marazion

16b.　From the front of the church, cross the road and walk down Eglos Road. Head out of the village until the road takes a sharp left. Now leave the road and walk straight ahead, along an unmade drive. As the drive turns right, walk ahead onto a footpath. Follow this footpath between some fields then cross a small drive and head into the next field. Cross this field bearing left and exit via a stile.

17b. The path now continues between several fields. Ignore all turnings until you cross a small stream. After the stream turn left and walk down the path that runs alongside Tremenheere Sculpture Gardens. When the path joins the Gardens' drive, head down to the main road and turn right.

18b. Walk along the road until you pass a left-hand junction. Just after the turning keep an eye on the right-hand hedge for a footpath. There is a flight of granite steps leading up off the road. Take this footpath and then walk along the next few fields, shadowing the road. Rejoin the road as the footpath climbs down some granite steps. You are now in the village of Gulval.

19b. Head towards the **Gulval Church** taking the left-hand junction. When you are in front of the church, cross the road, head through the lychgate and walk through the cemetery. Exit at the bottom on the left, join the road and turn right. This road can be busy and has no pavement. At the T-junction, cross the road and then walk forward, passing a set of concrete bollards. At the next T-junction cross the A30 at the traffic lights. Head towards the flyover and cross the train tracks. You are now on the South West Coast Path.

20b. Turn left and walk the two miles towards **St Michael's Mount**. This is a shared-use path with cyclists, so listen out for bells. You can make your way over to the island either by boat (there is a fee) or causeway, depending on the tide. This is the end of the walk.

St Michael's Mount / Marazion to Lelant

OS Maps: 102

WCs: All facilities at Marazion. Partial facilities at Lelant, Carbis Bay & Ludgvan

Length: 10 or 12.5 miles, depending on southern route

Link: https://cornishwalks.com/gpx-saints/

The southern section of the St Michael's Way has an east and west route meeting at Ludgvan. Read ahead to see which route you would prefer. If you want to collect the pilgrim stamps you will need to take the western route.

DIRECTIONS:

WESTERN ROUTE

0–4 miles: Marazion to Ludgvan

1. This walk starts at Marazion Station Car Park, just west of Marazion itself. Head to the far right of the car park facing the sea and continue along the path for two miles. This is a shared-use path with cyclists, so listen out for bells. When you reach the pedestrian flyover, head over the railway line then walk towards the traffic lights and cross the A30. Head up a small residential lane and at the crossroads continue straight ahead, following the road signs to Gulval. This section is on the road and can be busy.

2. When you get to the village turn right in front of **Gulval Church**, walk past a triangular patch of grass and take the footpath on the left. You need to climb

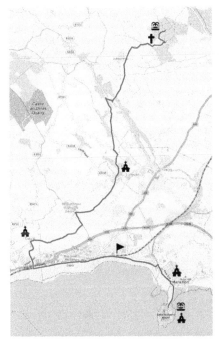

MARAZION TO TRENCOM (WEST)

73

a few steps up through the hedgerow. Follow the footpath through the next few fields as it shadows the road and then, at the corner of the last field, take the steps on the right back down onto the road. Continue along the road and turn left at the junction, towards Tremenheere Sculpture Garden.

3. Just before the entrance to the Gardens, take the wooden gate to the right-hand side and follow the footpath. Continue past the garden buildings on your left and then take a small wooden footbridge over the stream on your right. The path is clearly laid out through the next set of fields. When the track seems to split by some old buildings, take the upper left-hand fork. Continue along the path as it heads towards **Ludgvan Church**.

4. As the path turns into a small lane, head uphill then turn left at the T-junction. When you get to the church take the footpath to the left of the church.

EASTERN ROUTE

0–1.5 miles: Marazion to Ludgvan

1. From any of the car parks, head away from the sea, cross the road and walk towards Green Lane. Walk along Green Lane, taking the left-hand turning. Immediately after you cross a stone bridge, take the footpath to the right, heading down onto the Marazion marshes.

2. Follow the footpath through the marshes: at one point you will cross the main London train line. There are no barriers, so take care. The footpath is interrupted by a fast road. Cross with care and then take the path in front of you into a field.

3. Walk up three fields, keeping the hedge on your right, then exit via a stile at the top right. You now need to cross another road via the traffic island. Again, this is

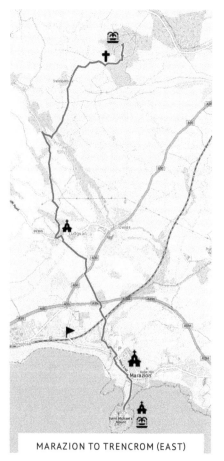

MARAZION TO TRENCROM (EAST)

a busy road. Once across, turn right and then left, following the sign to Ludgvan. When you reach a small industrial unit, take the footpath opposite.

4. Head up the field, keeping the hedge on your right. Cross a small lane then continue walking up the next field until the path ends at a road. You are now in Ludgvan. Turn left and walk towards the church.

The two routes are now joined.

Ludgvan to Trencrom Hill: 3 miles
5. Head around to the church tower then take the footpath that runs to the left-hand side. Follow the path down through woodland, across a small stream and then up to a small lane. Turn left and after a short distance take the footpath on the right, through a hedge. Keep to the left-hand side of this field. Head across the granite steps into the next field, then walk down towards the exit at the other end of the field in the bottom right corner. Ignore the gap in the hedge, which leads to another field, and exit via a wooden stile into a small, wooded area.

6. Follow the path, then cross another pretty stream and head uphill, veering left towards the hedgerow at the top of the hill. Exit via the gate at the top, and then in the next field stick to the left-hand side. When the path joins the road turn left and head downhill until you get to a sharp right-hand turning.

Take this turning and continue down until you reach a ford.

7. Just after the ford take the left-hand unmade drive. As the drive veers right take the left-hand path and walk up to the wooden stile. Now head uphill and exit via a wooden stile. This section is short but steep and can be slippery.

8. The path now crosses a set of nine fields. **Field 1:** head uphill keeping to the right-hand side. Exit via wooden gate. **Field 2:** walk across middle of the field towards a wooden gate and exit. Cross a small drive and head through a wooden gate. **Field 3:** walk directly across the field towards wooden gate and exit. Cross a small footpath and up to next wooden gate. **Field 4:** head directly across the field towards a metal gate. **Field 5:** head slightly right towards the first telegraph pole on your left. Exit via a wooden gate and cross a small lane towards another wooden gate. **Field 6:** walk directly across the field towards a wooden gate and exit. You should now get a clear view of Trencrom Hill over to your right. **Field 7:** walk directly across the field, heading towards a wooden post in the hedge. You should then see the wooden gate to exit. **Field 8:** turn right and walk diagonally across the field towards the telegraph poles then exit through a small metal gate. **Field 9:** head left and cut diagonally across the field, exiting at a small gate.

9. Follow the footpath as it cuts in front of a row of cottages. As you walk along by a small stream, if you look to your left you will see a small Celtic cross. You will need to walk through a private garden at this point, before the path joins a small road. Turn left and walk uphill and then take the right-hand fork. At the junction turn right and walk until you reach a small National Trust car park.

Trencrom Hill to Knill's Monument: 2.5 miles

10. There are now two options.

Route 1. If you want to climb the hill and explore the great views, head left and take any of the paths up to the top. Having enjoyed the views, make your way down off the hill heading right until you reach the road. Cross the road and find the footpath by a farm gate and granite stile. Depending on which path you came off the hill on, you may need to turn right or left along the road.

Route 2. If you want to avoid climbing **Trencrom Hill**, from the car park take the path to your right marked for the St Michael's Way. Follow this path until it ends at a small metal gate. Head through the gate until you reach a small lane. Turn left and walk up to a farmyard gate and a granite stile.

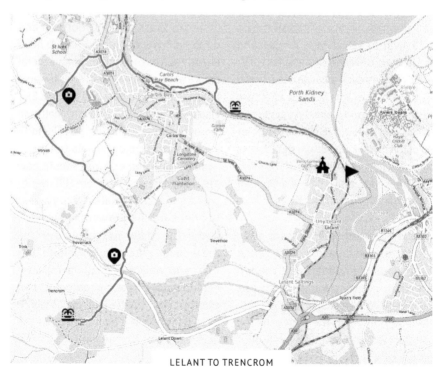

LELANT TO TRENCROM

11. Climb into the field and follow the path downhill, keeping the hedge to your right. At the bottom of the field exit right and then take a small path as it comes down to a road. Cross the road and walk up an unmade lane: to your left in a small meadow is **Bowl Rock**. Head up the lane until it ends at a cottage and then take the path to the right of the cottage. It may be obscured by a car.

12. Follow the path uphill and cross a stile into a wide grassy path. Walk forward with a field to your left and an equestrian centre to your right. Just before some large metal gates, climb through a gap in the hedge and once in the field turn right and walk to the corner of the field. Exit onto a road.

13. Cross the road and almost directly ahead take the lane into an agricultural yard. Just in front of the sheds, to the right-hand side, is a stile. Head into the field and then walk uphill, bearing slightly left. Your exit is to the left between two hedges. The path now heads through a development and exits onto a small road.

14. Turn left and walk for a mile until the road takes a sharp left. Take the footpath to the right and head up towards **Knill's Monument**, the large obelisk on the horizon. Enjoy the view from the top. It's pretty much downhill all the way now.

Knill's Monument to Lelant: 3 miles

15. From the monument, go straight ahead, take one of the paths onto the lane and walk downhill. Follow the lane for half a mile. At the T-junction at the end of the road turn right, and then at the second junction cross the A3074 in front of the Cornish Arms. Turn right. Just after the Carbis Bay sign take Wheal Margery on your left. This is the second turning after Manor Drive.

16. Head down Wheal Margery, as it bends to the right walk forward onto a pedestrian path. Look out for a metal handrail. Head down this path until you reach another. Turn right. You are now on the coast path and will follow this all the way to Lelant. Along this section the path passes St Uny's Holy Well. The route to the well is steep, slippery, hard to find and on the cliffside, so I don't describe it here.

17. Follow the path as you cross over the railway line and down through the Carbis Bay Hotel. Join the road and head uphill, keeping an eye out for the footpath on the left heading down towards the beach. Don't actually go down to the beach but stay on the coast path. Follow the path for 1.5 miles until you reach **St Uny's Church** at Lelant. This is the end of the walk.

Marazion Circular

OS Map: 102

WCs: All facilities at Marazion

Length: 6 miles

Link: https://cornishwalks.com/gpx-saints/

An excellent shorter walk making a loop of the east and west sections of St Michael's Way. There are great views at all points, no livestock and plenty of facilities along the way.

DIRECTIONS:

0–2.5 miles: Marazion to Gulval

1. This walk starts at Marazion Station Car Park, just west of Marazion itself. Head to the far right of the car park facing the sea and continue along the path for two miles. This is a shared-use path with cyclists, so listen out for bells.

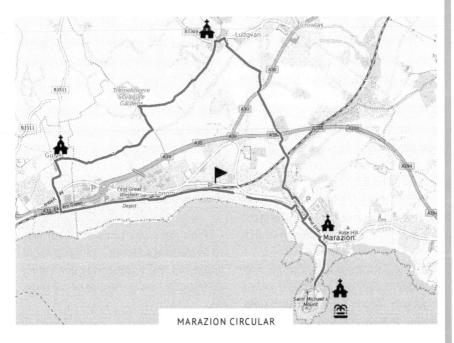

MARAZION CIRCULAR

When you reach the pedestrian flyover, head over the railway line then walk towards the traffic lights and cross the A30. Head up a small residential lane and at the crossroads continue straight ahead, following the road signs to Gulval. This section is on the road and can be busy.

2.5–4.5 miles: Gulval to Ludgvan

2. When you get to the village turn right in front of **Gulval Church,** walk past a triangular patch of grass and take the footpath on the left. You need to climb a few steps up through the hedgerow. Follow the footpath through the next few fields as it shadows the road and then, at the corner of the last field, take the steps on the right back down onto the road. Continue along the road and turn left at the junction, towards Tremenheere Sculpture Garden.

3. Just before the entrance to the Gardens, take the wooden gate to the right-hand side and follow the footpath. Continue past the garden buildings on your left and then take a small wooden footbridge over the stream on your right. The path is clearly laid out through the next set of fields. When the track seems to split by some old buildings, take the upper left-hand fork. Continue along the path as it heads towards **Ludgvan Church**.

4. As the path turns into a small lane, head uphill, continue uphill as it joins a larger road. At the T-junction, turn right, passing the church and then pass the

White Hart pub on your left.

4.5–6 miles: Ludgvan to Marazion

5. Just after the pub, on the opposite side of the road is a signpost for the St Michael's Way. Follow the path down through the fields, crossing a small lane as you go. When you reach the next road turn right. There is no footpath and the road can be busy. Follow the road towards a very busy T-junction then head up onto the grass verge to your right and walk over to the traffic island. Cross the road, turn right and then almost immediately take the left-hand stile into a field. Keep to the left of the three fields and exit at the bottom left.

6. At the bottom of the trees the path comes out onto a fast, busy main road. There is no traffic island. Cross with care and head straight onto the footpath ahead and away from the road. Follow the footpath through the Marazion marshes. At one point you will cross the main London train line. There are no barriers, so take care. As you arrive in Marazion, leave the footpath via a granite stile and head up onto a small road. Turn left, crossing a stone bridge, and then head towards the beach.

7. From here you can make your way to **St Michael's Mount** – either by boat (there is a fee) or causeway, depending on the tide. This is the end of the walk.

ST MICHAEL'S WAY: POINTS OF INTEREST

Granite Crosses

Always Christian symbols, these stone crosses come in a variety of shapes: lantern crosses, wheel crosses, four-holed crosses and so on. Crosses had a few uses but the two main ones were churchyard crosses to demarcate graveyards, and wayside markers. These markers were placed to help walkers travel to church or cross country, and they would mark the safest and easiest route. There are the remains of one on the St Michael's Causeway, essential as the tide turns.

Holy Wells

Mostly pre-Christian, these wells mark naturally occurring springs, many of which are still flowing. These wells are often associated with local folklore and pagan worship, as churches were often built alongside wells in an effort to combine the old and new religions. You may find scraps of coloured ribbons tied to branches around the well. These are known as clooties and act as prayers and offerings. You may also see painted stones and candles. As you can see, these wells are still a place of worship today and you should not take anything from these sites.

Mining

Cornwall's oldest and wealthiest industry has always been mining. The county is incredibly rich in metal and mineral deposits, which have fuelled Cornwall's history. As you walk you will see remnants of the tin, copper and clay mining industries. Beyond these major deposits, Cornwall was also rich in gold, uranium, arsenic, cadmium, lead and zinc. Even today, people are exploring lithium mining.

During the global industrial revolution it was said that at the bottom of a mineshaft anywhere in the world you would find a Cornishman showing the locals how to mine. Due to its geography, the rocks in the soil and the sea that surrounds it, Cornwall was easily the most cosmopolitan area of Britain, with global connections from every mine and port. The Cornish were global exporters of skills, intelligence and commodities.

St Uny's Church, Lelant

The start and finish point. There are some excellent gravestones in the church; the one with multiple suspicious deaths tells a tale. And be sure to visit the heritage centre, across the way in the other graveyard.

Knill's Monument

The monument was built as a mausoleum to John Knill, mayor of St Ives, in 1782. He made it the site of a regular festival to St James the Apostle. Ten young dancing girls from local fishing families, all dressed in white, went up and performed the Furry Dance, which was a local tradition. This would be played by a fiddler and the girls would be accompanied by two widows dressed in black. This celebration takes place every five years and is still performed today. Knill was eventually buried in London. The motto on the monument reads 'Resurgum': *I shall rise again*. Which seems fitting after the long walk up the hill.

Trencrom Hill

This is the site of an Iron Age hillfort. There is a spring on the western edge of the rocks, which is often referred to as the Giant's Well. It's hard to find, but if you locate a small gate and an electric fence you are there: the well is at the foot of the boulders. Trencrom was also said to be the home of the giant Trecobben, who often fought with **Cormoran**, the giant who lived at St Michael's Mount. Near the northern edge of the hill is **Bowl Rock**, which is said to have been dropped during a game between the two giants.

Trencrom Hill can also be considered a 'Mount Joy', a mediaeval term for the site where you can first see your destination. The term comes from Mount Joy, a hill outside of Jerusalem where pilgrims would get their first sight of the holy city. From Trencrom Hill you can see both ends of the walk.

Cormoran and Jack the Giant Killer

Cormoran was a giant who lived on St Michael's Mount and plagued the local villagers when he wasn't fighting with Trecobben. The Penzance elders offered a reward to anyone that could rid them of the giant. Up steps a young lad called Jack, who swam across to the island to lay a trap. He built a pit and tricked Cormoran into it. The foolish giant fell into the pit leaving only his head poking out the top. Jack then attacked his head with a pickaxe and Cormoran was no more. The pit is still visible today as a well on the island.

In another, kinder version, Cormoran lives to old age and is fed by Tom the Tinkeard.

Ludgvan Church

A beautiful church and the resting place of two well-known Cornishmen: William Borlase and Humphrey Davy. There is an impressive grave slab for John South (d.1636) as well as a carved figure of a man above the entrance to the church – an early monk, a pilgrim like yourself or even Saint Ludewon. Along with Towednack Church, Ludgvan claims to be the last place to have held mass in Cornish, in the late sixteen hundreds.

Gulval Church

Within the parish boundary lies Ding Dong mines, the oldest mines in Cornwall, and possibly Britain, which have been mined since prehistoric times. The rumour goes that Joseph of Arimathea came here as a trader and brought the young Jesus with him. There isn't a shred of evidence to support this claim, but it is a recent myth. Maybe William Blake was onto something in his poem, *Jerusalem*, when he asked, 'And did those feet in ancient time, Walk upon England's mountains green.' Are you walking in the footsteps of greatness?

The Church of St Michael and All Angels, St Michael's Mount

The beginning and end of your walk. Perched high on the island, there has been a church here from at least 1135, which was rebuilt in the fourteenth century.

Access to the chapel and island is ticketed, so check their website for details. The organ used to reside in London, where the insomniac owner would play it at night. At the request of his long-suffering neighbours, he sold it to the fifth Sir John St Aubyn in 1811.

The chapel is one of two pilgrimage locations in Cornwall, the other being St Petroc's Church at Padstow. The island has been in the ownership of the St Aubyns since the sixteen hundreds and still is today.

Saint Michael

Michael is one of the archangels and is associated with high places and slaying dragons. He is also one of Cornwall's patron saints and the patron saint of fisherman: a clear choice for Cornwall.

SURFING WITH THE SAINTS

A fabulous walk that follows in the footsteps of **St Piran**, one of Cornwall's patron saints, in and around Perranporth and Holywell. Along the way, the trail reveals lots of hidden places that are easily overlooked: sea caves, geological wonders, hidden lakes, ancient theatres and churches lost in the dunes. All this and a great choice of pubs.

Additional Information: This walk is best done at low tide and in good weather. The cliff section will be arduous or even dangerous in heavy rain, strong winds or low visibility.

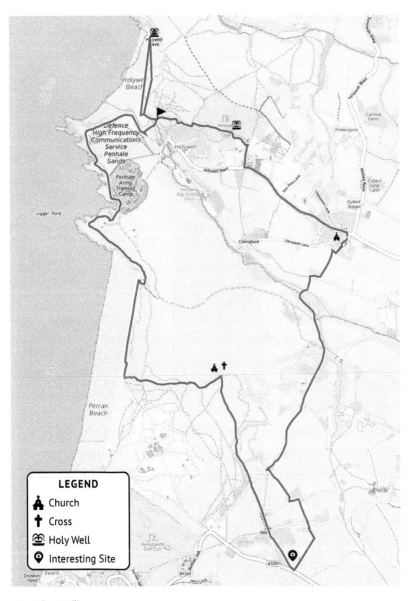

LEGEND

⛪ Church
✝ Cross
♨ Holy Well
📍 Interesting Site

Elevation Profile

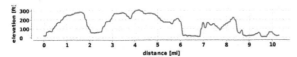

SURFING WITH THE SAINTS

OS Map: 104

WCs: All facilities at Holywell & Cubert

Length: 10 Miles. Effort: Strenuous

Link: https://cornishwalks.com/gpx-saints/

DIRECTIONS:

1. From the Holywell National Trust car park walk along the road back past the loos and up towards the seasonal convenience shop. Take the small road in front of the shop and follow the footpath signs. Turn right and follow the path along the perimeter of the houses. As you walk through the dunes stick to the main path, keeping to the edge of the houses. The path stops at a golf course. Rather than walk onto the course, take the path to the right of the gate. This cuts through scrubland and eventually you will pop out at a small intersection. To your left is a flight of concrete steps, ignore these and walk straight ahead until you emerge into a small glade with **St Cuthbert's Holy Well** on your left.

2. With the holy well behind you, walk past the pond and, with extreme care, out onto the golf course. Walk up the hill, sticking closely to the hedge on your right. You will see the flag for the 18th hole ahead and above you. Any ball coming in will be coming from the left – this is only a pitch and putt but still, take care. Continue past the green, through the large stone-lined gap in the hedge and walk straight towards the clubhouse. There is no charge to visit the well but there is a charity box in the reception, and a small donation may be appropriate. Leave the golf club and head out to the main road. Turn left and walk uphill to the village of Cubert – there is a pavement the whole way – and into the churchyard.

3. From the church tower, head out through the metal kissing-gate and take the left-hand footpath. When you reach the road, cross over, turn right, walk a few metres along the road and then walk down the next footpath. At the end of the footpath turn right and at the end of the passage, climb left through the stile into the field.

4. The view up here is amazing and

gives you an idea of the size of Penhale Sands. Walk down the field approximately halfway, keeping the hedge on your immediate right. The path then heads into the undergrowth and continues downhill through trees.

5. Follow the path until it pops out on a small track. There is a little slip path to the right, down onto the road. Take this path, and once on the road turn right and walk past Old Tree Barn on your left. At the end go through the second five-bar gate and turn left, continuing downhill until you reach the valley floor and stream. This whole area is a wetland and is likely to be very boggy in wet weather. Cross the bridge and continue along the path. Go through the kissing-gate and head left.

6. Soon the path comes out onto a large common and continues around its edge. The footpath is initially unclear, but stick to the left-hand edge of the common, skirting the scrubland. You are heading towards the electricity pylons on the skyline. After a short while, the path ends at a gate.

7. Head through the metal gate out onto a lane, turn right and walk uphill. This is a quiet lane, and while cars do use it, they are slow and there is plenty of room on the verges if you need to step off the road. Walk for about a mile until you reach a white bungalow on your left and the sign for 'The Wainhouse'

and 'Two Hoots Barn' on your right. Walk up the drive towards the bungalow and directly before the white gatepost turn right, following the footpath sign.

8. Follow this footpath into an arable field. Keep the hedge on your immediate right and walk the length of the field, heading towards the farm buildings. Just before the buildings, turn right down the track and then take the drive left. This will now bring you to the front of the farm buildings. Now walk downhill, climbing over the stile by the farm gate and continue down the drive.

9. Follow the drive down to the small road, cross over following the footpath sign and continue on the footpath, heading up alongside a cottage called Rose Wollas on the right. The footpath eventually ends at a large track opening into some fields. Turn right and follow the obvious track all the way until just before the road. There is a wooden fence to your right; climb over the stile and you will find yourself at the mediaeval amphitheatre of **Perran Round**.

10. Having explored the amphitheatre, you can now exit via the main gate and turn immediately right down an unmade road, through the village of Rose. Where the unmade road joins a tarmacked road, turn right and walk out of the village. You are now heading directly towards **St Piran's Oratory**. This road ends at a

T-junction where directly ahead and slightly to the right is a stile in the hedgerow. Head over the stile.

11. Once over the stile take the right-hand fork and walk into the **sand dune** system. There are many paths that you can take through here; however, you need to be moving in a right-hand direction, and sticking to the larger paths will achieve this. There are white-painted breezeblocks on the ground along the way. Follow these and take the right-hand branch when they split off. As you walk along you will gradually see a large modern cross on the horizon, keep this to your left.

The first feature you will come to is an ancient cross and a sunken church. Standing facing the information plaque, turn immediately left and follow the path downhill. Again, follow the white breezeblocks and cross over the small wooden bridge; within a minute you will come across the excavated **St Piran's Church Oratory**. First impressions are of an abandoned breeze block garage. Up to your left, towering over the landscape is the giant cross.

12. From either the large cross or the Church Oratory, you need to walk forwards towards the sea. You may come across a Ministry of Defence (MOD) fence – do not attempt to cross it. Instead, head down towards the beach. The descent is sandy and steep but good fun. Once on the beach turn right and walk to the far end. You are now on the coast path. In the far corner of the beach is a sea cave and lake. If you explore the lake area you can see some sealed-off shafts into a disused **mine**.

13. Leaving the cave behind, return to the coast path and start walking up the dunes. This is steep and tiring but soon you will be at the top with glorious views. Now stick to the coast path with the sea on your left. The next section needs to be walked with care; children and dogs need to be kept under control as you pass fenced-off mine shafts, exposed cliff edges and MOD land. This section is about two miles long and drops down into Holywell Bay.

14. Look across Holywell Bay to **St Cuby's Holy Well**, located in a sea cave. It is at the far side, to the right of an outcrop of rocks. If you would like to go and look at this cave, continue along the coast path and turn left onto the beach just before the St Piran pub. It is spectacular but be aware of the tide. It will only be accessible on a low tide.

15. From the beach return to the road and turn right, back towards the car park.

SURFING WITH THE SAINTS: POINTS OF INTEREST

Saint Piran

Piran, also known as Perran, was an Irish saint who was thrown out to sea by the Irish, tied to a millstone. As it hit the water, the waters stilled and so he rode upon the millstone across the Irish seas and landed on the north coast of Cornwall, making him the first known Cornish surfer. He is also credited with rediscovering the smelting of tin, thereby creating the symbol of the Cornish flag: the white molten tin crossing the black granite smelting block. St Piran's Day is celebrated on 5 March and is generally well celebrated throughout the county.

St Cuthbert's Holy Well

Tucked in the middle of a golf course is this pretty holy well. Believed to have been built in the fifteenth century, it was restored to its former glory in 1936. It is a beautiful spot sitting beside a range of ponds with the natural spring flowing down through the well.

St Cuby's Holy Well

As you walk around the headland and first look down on Holywell Bay, there is a sea cave dead ahead of you, on the other side of the beach. It is here that the holy well, from which the bay gets its name, is located. The cave is easy to

reach at low tide but impossible at high tide. There are no lifeguards at that end of the beach so always pay attention to the tide. To find the cave simply walk along the base of the cliff until you reach it. The well is on the left-hand side, above your head. It is not too far in and easy to see. As long as you are in the right cave!

This well appears to have taken advantage of a natural geological formation, where fresh water running down through the cliffs has created a natural spring and also left a variety of mineral deposits. These deposits have turned the surrounding rocks into a multicoloured splendour as well as forming shelves of calcium: it is a beautiful sight. Below the well there are steps leading up to it, but these are incredibly slippery and it is probably best to admire from afar rather than slipping and breaking something. When I visited, the well was high above me due to there being little sand in the cave. You may visit when the floor level is much higher. The existence of the well has been mentioned since 1685, when the Cornish historian William Hals remarked on its fame and curative properties.

Perran Round

This circular mediaeval amphitheatre

is known as a Plen-an-gwary, a Cornish open-air theatre used for the staging of miracle plays. Perran Round is considered the oldest and best-preserved example of its kind. You can still see the Devil's Pan in the centre, which would have been used to symbolise the descent into hell. This site was probably an earlier Iron Age enclosure.

Sand Dunes

Penhale Sands are the largest complex of sand dunes in Cornwall and are a designated Site of Special Scientific Interest. They are stabilised by marram grass, the malevolent spiky grass that stabs away at your legs and your will to live. Once this grass is established, other species begin to take root, further stabilising the sands. Penhale Sands is also the site of the mythical Langarroc, a village that was swallowed by the sands. Legend has it that on windy nights you can still hear its church bells tolling.

St Piran's Church, Oratory and Cross

The fact that the cross, St Piran's Church and St Piran's Oratory were all lost to the sands shows how easily the tale of Langarroc could be believed. The Oratory is thought to have been built in the sixth or seventh century and was founded by St Piran, which makes it one of the oldest surviving Christian sites in the UK. The encroaching sands meant that the local parishioners decided to build a

new church; they abandoned the Oratory and moved the cross to its current site. The church was then in use up until the nineteenth century, when again the battle against the sand was lost. A third church was then built five miles inland.

Ironically, having been regularly resurrected from the sands during the eighteenth and nineteenth centuries, the council reburied the Oratory in the 1980s to protect it from vandalism. The Oratory was once again resurrected in 2014. Sadly, the little church is now entombed behind iron railings and concrete blocks.

St Piran's Church, possibly dating from the twelfth century is now merely an outline in the ground, but it is at least accessible, and beside the site sits an ancient cross dating from 980. The church itself was eventually abandoned in the 1800s as the fight against the sands became impossible. Most of the church was torn down and re-used at the site of Lambourne, three miles away.

Mines

Sometimes it's hard to spot a place in Cornwall that doesn't have a mine. This mine was known as Gravel Hill. It was worked from the seventeenth century until 1882, producing iron and zinc. The shafts, spoil heaps, buildings and trackways associated with this mine are visible on vertical aerial photographs of the area.

CORNISH LANGUAGE

The words you see and hear in Cornwall look very different to the rest of England. This is because Cornwall once had its own language, which was in use up until the 1700s and only finally died out in the 1800s. The Cornish language is part of the Celtic family and shares many similarities with Welsh and Breton. In fact, many Welsh speakers recognise a lot of Cornish place names and sayings from their own language.

Today, Cornish is being spoken once more, and although there are no native speakers yet the language is all around you. The Cornish dialect has developed through a blend of two languages, English and Cornish, which means that things aren't always pronounced the way you might expect.

This quick little guide should help you through some of the more popular sayings and words, and help with translation of some of the place names.

Dialect

Aw right/alright – Hello, how are you. The response is, 'aw right, you?'

Backalong – Sometime in the past.

Brock – Badger.

Cousin Jack (Jill) – This was the name given to Cornish men (and women) who went to work in the mines overseas. It is also the name given to a certain type of stone wall where the topping stones stand up like jagged teeth.

Crib – Mid-morning snack. St Austell brewery has recently resurrected the factory whistle blowing at ten every morning, signalling a crib break for the workers. The steam whistle can be heard over a great distance.

Dreckly – This means I'll get around to doing that soon. It's been likened to the Spanish mañana but it's not so urgent!

Furze – Gorse. The lovely bright yellow spiky bush that blooms all year round in Cornwall.

Geddon – Lots of meanings for this one depending on where you are, and the context of the sentence. Are you joking? That's incredible. Hello. Goodbye.

Heller – A child throwing a proper tantrum.

Lover – Friendly greeting. Alright, lover. Can be used with a total stranger, male or female.

Mizzle – Not quite mist or rain but certainly wet.

Ope – A small little alleyway.

Proper Job – This is excellent.

Right on – I agree with you.

Some – Very. It's some hot, some wet, some busy.

Teasy – Tearful, fretful.

Up North, Away, Up Country, Foreigner – Basically, all these phrases refer to anyone or anywhere past the River Tamar.

Wasson – What's On? What's going on?

Cornish Words

The Cornish language is most visible in the placenames. There is a little rhyme that notes how much the language is still in effect in Cornwall.

> *By their names Tre, Pol, Pen, ye shall know the Cornishmen.*

If you look at the list below you can work out what a lot of local towns and villages mean.

Bos/Bod – home or dwelling.

Carn – a pile of rocks.

Cos – a forest, a wood or group of trees.

Eglos – meaning church.

Hayle – an estuary.

Lan – a sacred enclosure such as a church, monastery etc.

Maen (Men) – a stone.

Pen – an end of something, a headland or head.

Perran – named after St Piran/St Perran, the patron saint of tinners.

Pol – a pool.

Porth (Port) – a bay, port or harbour.

Ros – a moor, heath, or common.

Ruth – red.

Towan – sand dunes.

Tre – a homestead and its nearby buildings, literally a town.

Venton/Fenton – a spring or fountain.

Wheal – a mine.

FURTHER READING

Andy Bull (2021) *Pilgrim Pathways: 1–2 Day Walks on Britain's Ancient Sacred Ways.* Trailblazer Publications.

Nigel Marns (2017) *A Cornish Celtic Way.* Saysomething Artbooks.

Nicholas Orme (2018) *Medieval Pilgrimage: With a survey of Cornwall, Devon, Dorset, Somerset and Bristol.* Impress Books.

Recommended websites

https://www.csj.org.uk/caminos-in-the-uk

https://trurodiocese.org.uk/faith-life/pilgrimages/

https://britishpilgrimage.org/

https://www.cornwallheritagetrust.org/

https://www.nationaltrust.org.uk/

https://www.cornishmining.org.uk/

MORE BY LIZ HURLEY

To discover more of Cornwall try one of the following guides books, with more on their way.

CORNISH WALKS SERIES

WALKING IN THE MEVAGISSEY AREA
9780993218033 | https://amzn.to/2FsEVXN

WALKING IN THE FOWEY AREA
9780993218040 | https://amzn.to/2r6bDtL

WALKING WITH DOGS BETWEEN TRURO AND FOWEY
9780993218057 | https://amzn.to/2jd83tm

TOP WALKS IN EAST CORNWALL
9780993218088 | https://amzn.to/2XeBNZf

TOP WALKS IN MID CORNWALL
9780993218064 | https://amzn.to/2LTxUI8

CORNISH CYCLE RIDES
9781913628055 | https://amzn.to/3uNwJy9

AUTHOR'S NOTE

Like any good walking guide, this book has a long and rambling start. My children have both walked the Saints' Way in its entirety, when they were in primary school. Their very smart headmaster felt the best way to deal with exuberant year sixes, who have just finished their SATs, was to take them on an adventure. Like you, they did the walk in two days and parents often tagged along. This was the first time I walked the Saints' Way.

Fast forward to 2020, when I suggested to a group of friends that we walk the path. It was during one of the windows between lockdowns when we could manage to be together, and all Covid-19 restrictions were observed. A friend mentioned that she was fundraising for her son's charity, the Charlie Sumption Memorial Fund (CSMF), and so we walked to raise money in his memory. It felt poignant to walk this route that I had discovered with my own children. However, the charity is very much a celebration of his life and supports children at the Mutunyi School, in Kenya. To read more about the CSMF please visit this site.

https://www.csmf.co.uk/

The walk sparked new friendships and a group of us now walk regularly. It also made me realise that there was no guidebook in print that just focussed on the Saints' Way. As a writer of walking guides I figured I may as well fix that. And here it is, although it grew to include two other walks as well and I loved walking every mile of them. Although some of the hills tested my patience. And my lungs.

I am grateful for everyone who walked the paths and tested my instructions including Alison Gunderson and Pat Smith as well as Steve, Thomas and Finn. I am also grateful to my editors Denise Cowle and Anna Gow for knocking the text into shape and for Stephanie Anderson for the fabulous layout.

Get involved

I hope that you've enjoyed exploring the paths. If you have, let me know or share a review online.

Getting to know my readers is really rewarding; I get to learn more about you and enjoy your feedback and photos. So it only seems fair that you get something in return. If you sign up for my newsletter you will get various **free downloads of walks** plus whatever else I am currently working on. Sometimes I am also looking for testers and beta readers. I don't send out many newsletters, and I will never share your details. If this sounds good, click on the following: www.cornishwalks.com

I'm also on all the regular social media platforms so look me up.

#cornishwalks
@walkingincornwall

Milton Keynes UK
Ingram Content Group UK Ltd.
UKHW050726210624
444311UK00008B/39